LANDSCAPES OF BATTLE
The Civil War

UNIVERSITY PRESS OF MISSISSIPPI

JACKSON AND LONDON

LANDSCAPES

OF BATTLE

The Civil War

PHOTOGRAPHS BY
David Muench

TEXT BY
Michael B. Ballard

The maps in this book were created by Maria Campbell Brent.

The historic photographs were reproduced from *The Photographic History of the Civil War,* edited by Francis T. Miller (Yoseloff, 1957); *Battles and Leaders of the Civil War: People's Pictorial Edition* (The Century Co., 1888): and *Harper's Pictorial History of the Civil War* (Fairfax Press, 1977).

LIBRARY OF CONGRESS CATALOGING-IN-PUBLICATION DATA

Muench, David.
    Landscapes of battle : the Civil War / photography by
David Muench; text by Michael Ballard.
        p.   cm.
    ISBN 0-87805-365-4
    1. United States—History—Civil War, 1861–1865—
Pictorial works.
2. United States—History—Civil War, 1861–1865—
Battlefields—
Pictorial works.   I. Ballard,
Michael B.   II. Title.
E468.7.M94 1988
973.7—dc19   88-14345
                                                    CIP

PHOTOS: Antietam (p.i), Gettysburg (pp. ii–v, viii–ix),
            Vicksburg (pp. vi–vii), Shiloh pp. x–xi). Gettysburg
            (xiv), Vicksburg (xvi)

Contents

Photographer's Preface

Walking the open fields and forests of these great battle sites of the American Civil War can be a pleasant, satisfying, compelling, and, to some, even a mystical experience. The battlefields are an empty stage for us all to walk upon and from which we try to conjure up the tragic and grizzly destruction that was our Civil War. When we see the lush scenic beauty of the battle sites, so carefully maintained and interpreted by the National Park Service, it is difficult to realize the courage and intensity of the participants, the carnage left when the weapons were silenced and the dust was settled. Those are horrors almost unimaginable to the present visitor.

The photographs in this portfolio collection are not intended to invoke intensity of action in the battles of the 1860s, but rather they are a personal impression of various aspects of each site from a twentieth century viewpoint. These are color representations of an open stage in the 1980s. For me as a freelance photographer, used to making personal impressions of the landscape of American wilderness through the lens of a large format camera, the well manicured battlefields became more and more symbolically significant. With each successive visit to the battlefield parks, I felt, increasingly, a distinct relationship to the cause, dedication, and sheer courage of fellow Americans one hundred and twenty-five years ago. The Shilohs and Gettysburgs and the Vicksburgs are more than empty stages upon which to focus one's memories: they are now sacred fields, celebrated—even revered—for what they are in American history—places where thousands of brave fellow human beings sacrificed their lives for the cause and ideals they held most dear in their nativeland.

The photographs in this color portfolio of contemporary work were made with a large format 4 × 5 Linhof Field Camera, using Ektachrome daylight 64 film. Exposure calculations were made with a Gossen Luna Pro meter. The focal length of lenses varied from 75 to 600 millimeters. Filtration was sparingly used, primarily to bridge a gap between what is seen and what the film actually records. A tripod was used in most instances for stability.

In essence, I hope these photographs will give a unique visual experience of the present that rekindles the spirit of important moments fixed in the past.

DAVID MUENCH
April 1988

Introduction

NO PERIOD IN U.S. history has captured the American imagination as much as the Civil War. Books about it are strong sellers, movies usually draw crowds, and the numbers of participants and spectators at battle reenactments is impressive. Individuals and companies alike continue to produce videocassettes on a wide range of related topics. Just what about the conflict accounts for its perennial appeal?

Much of the answer lies in the response of the war generation in the North and the South. Between 1865 and the turn of the century, organizations sprang up to enshrine memories and to memorialize the dead. The Grand Army of the Republic in the North and the United Confederate Veterans in the South emerged and developed into potent social and political forces. Members relived the battles at meetings and in memoirs. With the passage of time, bonds formed between both groups of veterans, for whom the shared experience overshadowed the differences that had originally prompted the fight.

On Decoration Day, eventually renamed Memorial Day, Southern women commemorated Confederate dead by placing flowers on their graves. Women in the North soon adopted the idea. In both regions, war heroes were honored by statues in town squares, in cemeteries, and in the national parks that had once been battlefields.

In the South, the Lost Cause movement gave direction to the old Confederacy's grief and sense of loss. Southerners countered the ravages of war by celebrating Confederate paladins and Southern values such as personal honor, states' rights, agrarianism, conservative Christianity, and the sanctity of the home and womanhood.

Oral and written remembrances passed from generation to generation. Time cloaked the Civil War in a romantic aura that spread from the South to the rest of the nation. Sympathy for the underdog was surely a contributing factor, together with the American passion for history in general and for military history and heroes in particular. At this writing, as the last decade of the twentieth century approaches, the legacy's power is apparent.

Ironically, problems with which the war generation failed to cope also fortified the conflict's heritage. The freedmen looked to the future for a niche in society. The civil rights revolution of the mid-twentieth century inevitably recalled the death of slavery a hundred years earlier.

The enduring appeal of the Civil War era has to do with tradition, the written record, natural predilections, and the course of postbellum black history, but more nebulous factors also play a part. Having united several times to oppose foreign enemies, Americans may feel a special fascination with the history of a confrontation that pitted them against each other. And perhaps interest in the war feeds upon itself by reinforcing in the subconscious mind a belief in the conflict's significance for subsequent events.

Fort Sumter, South Carolina, viewed from Confederate Fort Johnson

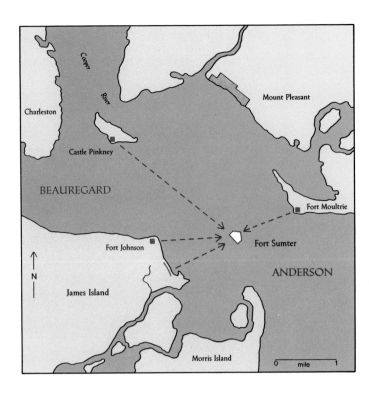

Fort Sumter   SOUTH CAROLINA

APRIL 12–14, 1861

SEVEN STATES IN THE Deep South seceded following Abraham Lincoln's election as U.S. president in November 1860. Southerners feared that Lincoln would interfere with the institution of slavery, a vital component of the South's economy and its social structure. After secession, coastline forts were seized to protect Dixie's commercial relations with the outside world, but a small garrison of fewer than one hundred Federal troops under Major Robert Anderson occupied Fort Sumter in Charleston Harbor, South Carolina, on December 26, 1860. South Carolina, the first state to secede, had not moved quickly enough to protect Sumter.

Anderson's action led to a loud debate between officials in Washington, D.C., and the newly formed government of the Confederate States of America. A battery manned by Citadel College cadets turned back a relief ship sent to the fort in January from New York. By the time Lincoln took the oath of office in March 1861, nothing had been resolved.

Meanwhile, Anderson and his men waited inside the fort named for South Carolina revolutionary War hero Thomas Sumter. The impressive pentagonal structure had brick walls five feet thick which rose some fifty

feet above low tide. The interior contained a parade ground about an acre in size. Two lower-level casemates (protected compartments for cannon) extended along four walls. The top level, the barbette, held several unprotected guns. Officers' quarters occupied the fifth wall, and a barracks three stories high paralled the gun emplacements. But the barracks were unfinished, and several casemates had no guns. When Anderson prepared for battle, he left the barbette unmanned and concentrated his small force around parade ground batteries and along the bottom tier of casemates. (The second-tier casemates had not been armed at all and were sealed.) By April 12, sixty guns were in place. The garrison constructed bomb shelters for protection from Confederate artillery, mined the wharf outside the fort, and erected overhanging galleries from which shells could be dropped by hand. Invaders could expect a hot reception.

By the end of March, Lincoln had decided to take decisive action. He would not order Anderson to evacuate, nor would he recognize the Confederacy. Another relief expedition would be sent at once.

On April 10, Confederate President Jefferson Davis sent word to General P.G.T. Beauregard, who commanded

Rebel forces at Charleston, that he should demand Anderson's immediate surrender. The next day Beauregard dispatched three aides to confer with Anderson, who had been Beauregard's artillery instructor at West Point. Anderson responded that a lack of supplies would force him to evacuate within a few days. Until that time, he could not surrender without orders.

Beauregard forwarded his reply: "If you will state the time at which you will evacuate . . . , we will abstain from opening fire upon you." Anderson received this note at 12:30 A.M. on April 12. The major conferred with his officers and then told Beauregard's aides that he would evacuate by April 15 unless otherwise instructed by Washington. This was not the definite answer that the Confederates sought, and so Anderson was notified at 3:20 A.M. that he would be fired upon in an hour.

U.S. soldiers watched the stream of light arching toward them from the west at 4:30 A.M. on Friday, April 12. Onward streaked the light, and then came the explosion. A ten-inch mortar shell had shattered over the center of the fort. With the firing upon Fort Sumter, the American Civil War had begun.

The first shell came from Fort

3

Johnson on James Island. It was followed by a barrage from forty-three cannon and mortars in batteries from Morris Island to the south, James Island to the west, and Mount Pleasant and Sullivan's Island to the northwest and north of Sumter. To save ammunition, Anderson ordered his troops not to man their guns until daylight.

At 7:00 A.M., the guns of Sumter began returning fire, and the battle began in earnest. The hail of Rebel shells falling inside the fort forced Anderson to rely on guns in the lower-tier casemates; As a result his field of fire was limited. Most shells bounced harmlessly off iron-covered Confederate batteries. One observer compared the Union cannon shot "to marbles thrown by a child on the back of a turtle."

In contrast, the Confederate bombardment had a devastating effect. During the first day's shelling, Sumter's barracks caught fire three times, ignited by heated shells from Beauregard's guns. Braving the whirlwind of iron, brave defenders extinguished the fires, but heavy Confederate artillery shattered the fort's walls and disabled two Yankee guns.

Outside Charleston Harbor, Lincoln's relief ships arrived early on Friday, but weather conditions and a confusion of orders involving one of the war ships forced the expedition to return to New York. Unaware that he had been left to his fate, Anderson continued to fight and to hope for reinforcements.

On Saturday morning, April 13, hot Confederate shells set officers' quarters ablaze. Heavy smoke blanketed the fort's defenders. During the early afternoon, the flagstaff was shot down. Seeing no flag, one of Beauregard's aides, without authorization from the general, rowed out to see whether Anderson was surrendering. Anderson was ready to give up the fight, and he agreed to terms. When aides actually sent by Beauregard arrived later, Anderson felt betrayed, but he agreed not to start fighting again if the original terms held.

Sunday morning, April 14, the Sumter garrison raised the Stars and Stripes one last time and fired a one-hundred gun salute. On the forty-seventh round, an accidental explosion killed Private Daniel Hough and wounded several others, one of whom died later. Despite all the heavy shelling, these two Union soldiers were the only fatalities of the battle. Hough was buried on the parade ground, and an emotional Anderson led his men out of the Sumter ruins to the tune of "Yankee Doodle."

The next day Lincoln issued a call for seventy-five thousand volunteers to suppress the Southern rebellion. Davis sent his vice-president, Alexander Stephens, to the state of Virginia, which had not yet seceded. Neither president knew what fate might have in store. For the time being, Lincoln needed men, and Davis needed Virginia. Before Sumter the concern had been how to avoid war; now both sides were taking steps to win it.

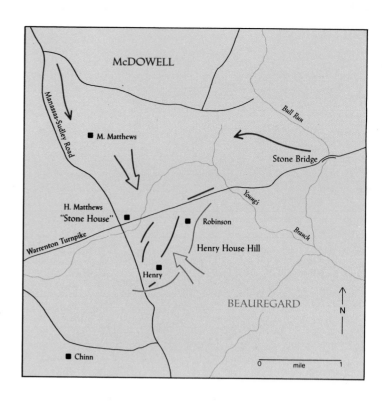

First Manassas   VIRGINIA

July 21, 1861

AFTER THE FALL of Fort Sumter, states rushed to choose sides. In May 1861, Arkansas, Tennessee, North Carolina, and Virginia joined the Confederacy. Kentucky and Missouri wavered. The former attempted neutrality; the latter had state governments representing both the Union and the Confederacy. Maryland, vital to the security of the U.S. capital, was occupied by Federal forces and was obliged to stay in the Union.

The transfer of the Confederate capital from Montgomery, Alabama, to Richmond, Virginia, set the stage for the first big battle of the war. With Richmond and Washington only a hundred miles apart, the Rebel capital became an obvious Yankee target. Cries of "On to Richmond" filled Northern newspapers and forced reluctant Union generals to invade Virginia with troops that were less than adequately trained.

On June 3, Winfield Scott, general-in-chief of the Union armies, ordered General Irvin McDowell to prepare for an attack against Confederates commanded by P.G.T. Beauregard at Manassas Junction, some twenty miles southwest of Washington. The idea was to beat Beauregard's twenty-three thousand troops before General Joseph E. Johnston's eleven thousand men at Winchester, Virginia, could come to the rescue.

General Robert Patterson's Union army at Martinsburg, Virginia, tried without success to keep Johnston's attention occupied. Johnston, having been alerted to McDowell's march on Manassas, left Winchester on July 18. Screened by J.E.B. Stuart's calvary, nine thousand Confederates moved eastward to join Beauregard. Not until two days later did Patterson realize what had happened.

Johnston's lead brigade, under the command of Thomas Jonathan Jackson, an eccentric professor at Virginia Military Institute, reached Beauregard in the afternoon of July 19. Most of Johnston's army arrived the next day. On July 18, the Federal army reached Centreville, just north of Manassas and Bull Run, a small, high-banked stream that ran northwest to southeast in front of Manassas. Like Johnston, McDowell had problems making time with raw recruits. Men stopped to pick blackberries or simply to rest. Even so, if McDowell had attacked immediately, Beauregard might have been whipped before Johnston arrived in force.

But McDowell waited, no doubt unsettled by the defeat of an advance detachment at Blackburn's Ford on the Confederate right flank. Rugged terrain and Rebel resistance on his

left persuaded McDowell to shift his offensive to the right. While McDowell pondered strategy, two days passed, and Beauregard's army grew larger. By dawn of July 21, McDowell no longer had the numerical advantage.

Joe Johnston, the senior Confederate general present, deferred to Beauregard's battle plan, which called for an assault against the Union left. With McDowell ready to hit the Rebel left, the two armies could theoretically go around in a circle if both attacks took place at the same time. The course of the fight would therefore depend on who struck first.

The sun rose on Sunday, July 21, illuminating a clear sky and promising hot temperatures. McDowell's First Division headed for a stone bridge that crossed Bull Run several miles northwest of Manassas. The Second and Third divisions crossed Bull Run to the right of Warrenton Turnpike and wheeled back to the left to deliver the main attack against the Rebel left. The Fourth Division waited in reserve except for one brigade that demonstrated on Beauregard's right at Blackburn Ford.

Shortly before 5:00 A.M., the First Division opened fire on Confederate general Nathan Evans's troops across the stone bridge. Evans correctly suspected that this was a diversion. He

Stone House, Manassas National Battlefield Park, Virginia

The crossing of Bull Run at Blackburn Ford was a prelude to the first great combat of the war.

kept an eye on his left while Beauregard began sending reinforcements. Beauregard realized that he had been beaten to the punch. The Confederate attack on the Yankee left was called off.

Beauregard needed time to shift his army, and he got it. McDowell's flank march had fallen behind schedule. The two Union divisions were to attack at 7:00 A.M., but not until 9:00 did Confederate observers warn Evans of large numbers of the enemy moving toward his left. The Rebels fought a delaying action and then retreated to high ground north of the turnpike.

At this point the battle began in earnest. Colonel Ambrose Burnside's brigade of the Second Division slammed in Evans's force. Reinforcements helped stabilize Evans's line, but if McDowell quickly brought more men forward, the battle could be won. Support soon came, but not at McDowell's bidding.

William T. Sherman pulled his men away from the stone bridge, crossed Bull Run, and charged Evans's right flank.

The Rebel line broke and retreated over Young Branch bottom, across the Warrenton Turnpike, and up the slopes of hills where the Henry and Robinson houses stood. Trying to reform his frightened men, General Bernard Bee was relieved to see General Jackson's command poised for combat just beyond the crest of Henry house hill. Jackson had moved toward the sound of battle and arrived in time to save the day. Bee yelled, "There is Jackson standing like a stone wall! Rally behind the Virginians!" Bee soon fell, mortally wounded, but his description of the general entered the annals of the war.

Although Jackson stemmed the Yankee tide, the battle was far from over. With much bloodshed but little advantage to either side, fighting ebbed

and flowed along the hillcrest for hours. Beauregard shifted the weight of his army to his left in an attempt to turn McDowell's right and force the Federals back toward Bull Run. As the battle raged into the afternoon, an approaching cloud of dust in their rear gave Beauregard and Johnston some anxious moments. Could it be Patterson coming to McDowell's rescue? The dust clouds came closer and closer. At last Beauregard recognized the friendly flag of Jubal Early's regiments. Early filed in on the left, and at last the Union right gave way.

The retreat of the Federal army was not initially marked by panic. The mixing of regiments, the nonregulation uniforms worn on both sides, and the similarity of the battle flags all added to the disorder; the collapse of the Union right flank only made matters worse. But Rebel shelling of retreat routes was probably responsible for the rout. Members of the capital bureaucracy had journeyed in their Sunday best to watch while the rebellion was crushed. They picnicked and partied and seemed to regard war as nothing more than a spectator sport until McDowell's army turned and ran. Then fine carriages raced dusty soldiers to see who could reach Washington first. The Confederates did not follow. In this springtime of the war, victory could leave an army as disorganized as defeat.

Casualties had been light compared with what was to come. In the Battle of First Manassas, called First Bull Run in the North, the Union lost fifteen hundred killed and wounded, the South eighteen hundred. Illusions of quick victory on both sides had also been a casualty. And perhaps innocent romance and glory had passed away with the demise of eighty-four-year-old Judith Henry, who asked to be returned to her sickbed in the heat of battle and died there when artillery shells crashed through the roof.

Henry House, Manassas

Stone Bridge, Manassas

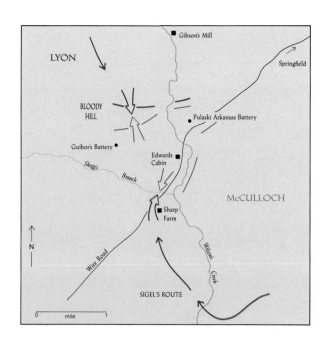

Wilson's Creek   MISSOURI

August 10, 1861

In missouri the debate over secession led to military action between Captain Nathaniel Lyon's Federal forces and pro-Confederate state troops led by Governor Claiborne Fox Jackson and General Sterling Price. Lyon seized the initiative early. By the end of June 1861, he had forced Price and Jackson into southwest Missouri. Confederate general Ben McCulloch marched his army up from Arkansas to reinforce the Missourians. McCulloch assumed overall command of the joint force of some eleven thousand men.

To oppose McCulloch, Lyon had only fifty-five hundred men, but the Union force had superior arms, equipment, and training. When Lyon learned that the Confederates were on the march toward his position at Springfield, he determined to attack.

On August 6, the Confederates camped along Wilson's Creek some ten miles southwest of Springfield. The creek ran northwest to southeast; the Rebel army occupied both banks in order to cover the Springfield-Fayetteville road, which gave the Federals an obvious approach route.

On Saturday, August 10, at daylight, the Union forces struck the Wilson Creek camp. Lyon rushed in from the north while a detachment under Franz Sigel marched around and attacked from the south. Inexperienced Confederate officers had posted no pickets. As a result many of their men were captured while they were leisurely eating breakfast.

News of the attack spread, but Price and McCulloch dismissed as camp gossip the initial reports that reached headquarters. A whirlwind retreat of men and animals from the north convinced them otherwise. Soon Federal artillery thundered at both ends of the camp. The two Rebel generals set about rallying their troops. The situation was not as desperate as it seemed; the stampede consisted largely of undisciplined cavalry and camp followers.

To the north, Confederate infantry quickly rallied and brought Lyon's charge to a halt. General J.H. McBride's Ozark mountaineers particularly distinguished themselves. With the line stabilized, Price began pouring regiment after regiment into the showdown with Lyon.

The storm center of the battle was a scraggly eminence called Oak Hill. By the time the fighting had ended, this spot had earned the name Bloody Hill. The body count grew because neither side could gain an advantage. As the stalemate lingered, troops charged and countercharged, both lines held, and casualties mounted. The key to victory would be Sigel's effort at the southern end of the Rebel line.

At first Sigel's men fought well. Surprised Confederates retreated before the attacking Federals, who, convinced that a victory had been won, stopped to plunder. McCulloch hurriedly sent a Louisiana infantry regiment and a Missouri cavalry battalion to counterattack. Here, as at First Manassas, the variety of uniform colors caused confusion. The Louisianans wore gray; so, too, did an Iowa regiment. The Confederates marched unharmed to close range and opened fire. Rebel artillery shelled Sigel's flanks, and his men either surrendered or scattered. Sigel escaped and rode hard back to Springfield.

McCulloch now joined Price's fight against Lyon. The combined Confederate forces began to make headway at last but only after more hours of hard fighting. Price fell wounded. Lyon died. Lyon's officers decided to retreat, leaving their commander's body in enemy hands.

The Yankees marched back to Springfield unmolested. McCulloch's army had exhausted most of its ammunition and was in disarray after the bitter fighting on Bloody Hill. On orders from Richmond, McCulloch soon went back to Arkansas, while Price moved on to Springfield, which the Federals quickly evacuated.

The battle at Wilson's Creek resulted in thirteen hundred Union and twelve hundred Confederate casualties. But all the bloodshed had settled nothing. More men would have to die before Missouri's fate was decided.

Wilson's Creek, Wilson's Creek National Battlefield, Missouri

On Bloody Hill, Wilson's Creek

Fort Donelson National Battlefield

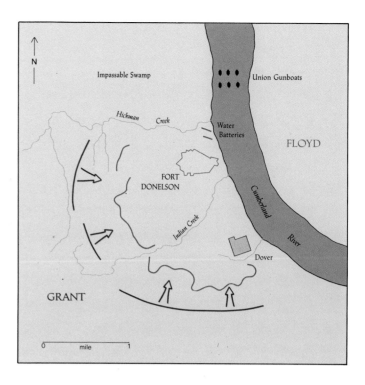

Fort Donelson TENNESSEE

FEBRUARY 13–16, 1862

WHILE THE CONFEDERATE government concentrated on the defense of Richmond, the preservation of the vast western Confederacy was left to the wiles of one man, General Albert Sidney Johnston. Johnston had too many miles to cover and too few men to get the job done. A Federal victory at Fishing Creek, Kentucky, on January 19, 1862 cracked the Rebel line that stretched precariously from eastern Kentucky to the Mississippi River. On February 6, Union forces under General U.S. Grant captured Fort Henry on the Tennessee River just south of the Tennessee-Kentucky state line. Grant's victory threatened Johnston's hold on Tennessee.

A few miles east of Fort Henry, across a narrow neck of land between the Tennessee and Cumberland rivers, lay Fort Donelson. Though his forces were scattered, Johnston decided to make a stand at Donelson. If the fort fell, Grant would have free passage to the vitals of the lower South.

Fort Donelson stood on the west bank of the Cumberland on high ground that gave its defenders a panoramic view to the north, the direction from which Federal gunboats would ascend. The fort encircled about fifteen acres and had been designed to provide infantry support for artillery batteries, which

numbered some twenty-five guns. On the land side, rifle pits were rushed to completion after the fall of Fort Henry. Overall the position was not impregnable, but if Johnston concentrated enough men, Grant would face a formidable task. Unfortunately for the South, Johnston effected no such concentration.

On February 11, Grant set his infantry in motion toward Donelson. Admiral Andrew Foote took his flotilla of gunboats and transports north to the Ohio River, then east to the mouth of the Cumberland. Along the way, he picked up ten thousand reinforcements for Grant, who would now have an advantage over the Confederates at Donelson of twenty-seven thousand to fifteen thousand men.

The battle for Fort Donelson began on Thursday, February 13, with an attack by Union General John McClernand on the Confederate left flank held by General Gideon Pillow's division. The fighting quickly spread. On the Federal left, General C.F. Smith's assault was repelled by General Simon Bolivar Buckner's Rebels. After the battle had started, Grant adjusted his lines to install General Lew Wallace's division in the center. Wallace's men were the reinforcements brought in by Foote.

The fighting throughout the day

was indecisive, though Confederates manning a big columbiad artillery piece scored a moral victory when one of the gun's huge shells disabled the Federal gunboat *Carondelet*. The weather turned nasty in the afternoon, sleet fell, and the temperature dropped to a low of ten degrees during the night. Shivering soldiers continued to shoot at one another after dark, but the real story of this night to remember was the suffering of the wounded. Many froze to death. A few burned in fires ignited by exploding artillery shells.

Two inches of snow fell on the landscape before the morning of February 14. Fighting waned on the land side of the fort.

On the river a raging cannonade developed between Foote's gunboats and Confederate batteries. Federal shot and shell beat down Rebel breastworks but did little damage to guns and crews. Meanwhile, Donelson's big guns effectively hammered away at Yankee boats. Foote's flagship, the *St. Louis*, received heavy damage. Foote and several of his crew were wounded. Finally the admiral ordered a retreat.

Despite encouraging results, the Confederate command had already decided to evacuate the fort. John Floyd, the general in command, was not a career soldier. It did not take much to

Buckner's Last Defense, Fort Donelson

River batteries on the Cumberland River, Fort Donelson National Battlefield, Tennessee

convince him that he could not hold out without thirty or forty thousand more men. In conference with Pillow and Buckner, Floyd agreed to a breakout plan.

Pillow would attack Grant's right and push open an escape route to the south toward Nashville. The operation began on Saturday morning, February 15, with a charge by Pillow's division. McClernand's division fell back, and the Federal right soon disintegrated. The way to Nashville was open. But Pillow kept charging, then stopped and, rather than leading a retreat, fell back to his original position! Grant shored up his line and ordered an assault on the Confederate right, which had been weakened by the concentration on the left for Pillow's attack.

Pillow's incompetence had wasted a tactical victory. Disheartened and convinced that Grant would continue to receive reinforcements, the trio of Confederate generals decided to surrender. If Sidney Johnston had really intended to make a stand at Donelson, he should have picked abler commanders; in fact, he should have come to the fort to take personal command. The Confederate soldiers here had put up a good fight, and now they would be rewarded with a trip to Northern prisons.

A few thousand of the fort's defenders did escape on a river transport, as did Floyd and Pillow. The intrepid Rebel cavalry commander Nathan Bedford Forrest led his men to safety during the night of February 15.

On Sunday, February 16, Buckner surrendered the fort to Grant. During the negotiations Grant wrote, "No terms, except unconditional and immediate surrender." Northern newspapers were soon praising the heroic "Unconditional Surrender" Grant. In capturing Donelson, Grant had lost some twenty-seven hundred killed and wounded, but his army had inflicted two thousand casualties and had bagged about nine thousand prisoners.

The way to the deep South's interior stood open. Johnston would have to abandon the Tennessee capital of Nashville. The city had never been properly fortified, and there was no time to do the job now. Johnston retreated, and the victorious Grant moved on down the Cumberland and Tennessee rivers. The two generals would soon meet again on the Tennessee at a port called Pittsburg Landing.

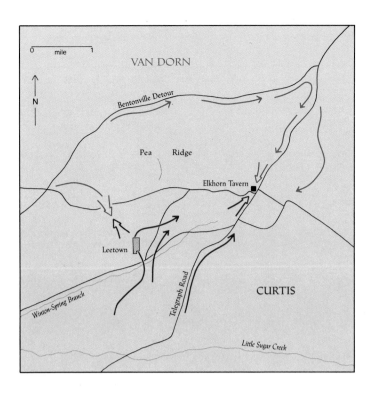

Pea Ridge ARKANSAS

MARCH 7–8, 1862

AFTER WILSON'S CREEK, the Confederate government named a new commander, General Earl Van Dorn, to take over the forces of Sterling Price and Ben McCulloch. Van Dorn envisioned the capture of St. Louis and even an excursion into Illinois both for his own glory and, more important from the standpoint of the South, to take pressure off Sidney Johnston's army in Tennessee.

The new Union commander in Missouri, General Samuel Curtis, took the initiative against Van Dorn by driving Price out of Springfield, Missouri, into northwest Arkansas. There, south of Bentonville, Van Dorn consolidated his force of some sixteen thousand and on March 4 moved to meet Curtis's eleven thousand camped near Fayetteville. The Federals retreated along Telegraph Road, the main thoroughfare of the area, to Sugar Creek, a stream that flowed east and west along the base of Pea Ridge (so named for the wild peas that grew on its slopes).

Curtis had taken a strong position, and so Van Dorn decided to march around the Yankees and attack them from their rear. An eight-mile trail called the Bentonville Detour would allow the Rebels to wheel to the left, circle Pea Ridge, and turn back into

Telegraph Road well north of Curtis's current position. If he was successful, Van Dorn could cut off both the Federal supply line and the retreat route.

On the night of March 6, Van Dorn began his flank march with Price's men leading the way. A night march with relatively inexperienced troops would have been difficult enough under ordinary circumstances. Van Dorn's failure to reconnoiter the trail made the army's advance even more difficult. Curtis knew of the detour and had ordered his men to obstruct the passage with trees. Van Dorn had also failed to have an adequate bridge built over Sugar Creek, which further delayed the march.

Curtis had time to begin shifting his force away from Sugar Creek toward Elkhorn Tavern, located north of the creek on Telegraph Road. To gain more time, Curtis ordered a detachment under Peter Osterhaus to attack the Rebel column as it passed along the detour west of the hamlet of Leesburg.

The night of delays kept Price from getting in position on the Telegraph Road north of Elkhorn Tavern until 10:00 A.M., Friday, March 8. Back along the detour, McCulloch had been stopped by Osterhaus's attack. With Van Dorn's approval, McCulloch launched a counterattack. This was a mistake on Van Dorn's part, for he would now be

in a two-front battle, with the lofty eminence of Pea Ridge separating the wings of his army.

Initially, the battle went well for the Confederates on both fronts. When Price attacked, Curtis had not yet brought all his men up from Sugar Creek. Price's superior numbers shoved the Yankees back south of Elkhorn Tavern, but as more Federals arrived, the Union line stabilized. The battle settled into a bloody shoving match in which Price soon fell wounded.

On the other battle front, McCulloch's advance had deteriorated into disaster. McCulloch had been killed, and so had his second in command, James McIntosh. Louis Hébert, the next in line, had been captured. Albert Pike, the inexperienced commander of an even less experienced group of Indians, was left in command. Pike's Indians were colorful and were anxious to fight for the Confederacy, but they panicked when Union artillery fired upon them. Lacking adequate leadership and with the Indians running away, McCulloch's division disintegrated. A few thousand survivors did manage to join Price's division before the fighting ended on Telegraph Road.

The Confederate debacle on his left allowed Curtis to concentrate all his attention on Price. During the first day's

Last hour of the Battle of Pea Ridge, Elkhorn Tavern at right

combat, the Federals had taken a severe pounding at Elkhorn Tavern, but the lines had held. Now the odds would be more even.

On Saturday, March 8, Van Dorn decided not to resume the attack on Price's front. McCulloch's defeat had shaken Van Dorn, and he seemed to have lost his fighting spirit. He had also lost a reserve ordnance wagon train that had been mistakenly directed away from the army. Curtis waited, then launched an attack of his own. Van Dorn ordered a retreat and the battle was over. The Federals made a feeble pursuit that quickly fizzled.

The Battle of Pea Ridge (or Elkhorn Tavern, as it was called in the South) signaled the end of Confederate threats to force Missouri out of the Union. But the reason was Sidney Johnston's predicament in Tennessee rather than Van Dorn's defeat. Johnston needed more men to fight U. S. Grant, and the Confederate government had decided that this effort had greater priority than securing Missouri. It could be argued that the Battle of Pea Ridge need never have been fought.

Elkhorn Tavern, Pea Ridge National Military Park, Arkansas

Winton Springs, Pea Ridge

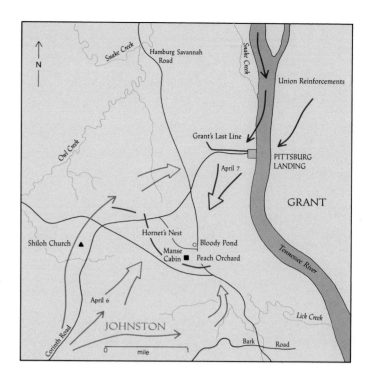

Shiloh TENNESSEE

APRIL 6–7, 1862

FOLLOWING THE FALL of Fort Donelson, Albert Sidney Johnston decided to concentrate his Confederate army at Corinth in northeast Mississippi. He knew that Grant's army, temporarily under the command of General C. F. Smith, had moved south from Donelson, had occupied Nashville, and was now coming south down the Tennessee River. On the advice of General William T. Sherman, transferred shortly after First Manassas from Virginia to the western front, Smith chose as his base of operations Pittsburg Landing, a site on the south bank of the Tennessee some twenty miles northeast of Corinth. The Federals planned to crush Johnston with a combined force of some seventy thousand men that included the armies of U. S. Grant and Don Carlos Buell. Johnston concluded that he must march his forty-four thousand troops against Grant at once. The Confederates would have a slight numerical advantage if the job could be done before Buell arrived from Middle Tennessee.

On Thursday, April 3, 1861, Johnston's army started for Pittsburg Landing. The attack would be made on Saturday morning. Muddy, narrow roads and the army's lack of marching experience forced Johnston to delay the offensive until Sunday.

The Federal army was camped along a line facing west and south a few miles inland from the Tennessee. A prominent landmark along the line was a small Methodist meetinghouse called Shiloh. The building stood by the main road from Corinth on the right center of Sherman's division. Owl and Snake creeks encircled the Union right to the north and northwest. On the left flowed Lick Creek, which emptied into the Tennessee south of the landing.

Johnston planned to strike hard at the Union left, pushing the Yankees away from Pittsburg Landing and driving them north into the swampy area of Owl and Snake creeks. The Confederate battle alignment did not conform to Johnston's strategy. He stacked the corps of Generals William Hardee, Braxton Bragg, and Leonidas Polk one behind the other. (John C. Breckinridge commanded a reserve corps.) With the army thus formed, Johnston faced the probability that in the heat of combat his army would strike evenly across the Union front rather than shifting its weight toward the targeted Federal left. And that is exactly what happened.

The battle began shortly before 5:00 A.M. on April 6 with a clash of pickets in front of Sherman's position. Sherman's division and the division on his left commanded by General Benjamin Prentiss received the brunt of the initial rebel attack.

The Federal command was not ready for battle. Grant, who had resumed command, was eating breakfast in Savannah, Tennessee, several miles to the northeast on the opposite bank of the river, when the battle of Shiloh got under way. Along the Union lines, a few early risers were preparing breakfast. Incredibly, even though they knew that Johnston was in Corinth, Grant and his subordinates had ignored picketing and patroling reports that should have warned them of the enemy's approach.

The Rebels attacked hard and fast, sweeping everything before them like a tidal wave, but the Confederates on the left advanced faster than those on the right. Johnston's strategy was in trouble right from the beginning. Sherman's division and John McClernand's division on Sherman's right fell back quickly under the pressure of Hardee's corps. The Rebels soon held the Shiloh area, but the Confederates succeeded in bending the Federal right back toward Pittsburg Landing, exactly what Johnston did not want.

Aware of the turn of events, Johnston rode toward the battle on the right to urge his men on. In a raging fight among the blossoms of a peach orchard, a bullet struck an artery in Johnston's leg. He died from loss of blood shortly afterward.

Tennessee River at Pittsburg Landing, Shiloh

P. G. T. Beauregard, veteran of Fort Sumter and First Manassas, took command of the army.

Through the night, Grant fed Lew Wallace's division and some twenty thousand of Buell's men into his battered line. Wallace, who would later write *Ben Hur*, had been camped at Crump's Landing several miles north of the battlefield. The additions gave Grant a numerical advantage of nearly twenty thousand when the battle resumed on Monday, April 7.

Beauregard's tired army fought well but slowly lost the ground that it had won the day before. Van Dorn never arrived, and Beauregard concluded by early afternoon that he must retreat back to Corinth. Grant offered little pursuit. His army had been chewed up, and he was glad to see the Rebels go.

Casualties at Shiloh (called the Battle of Pittsburg Landing in the North) staggered the divided nation. The Union lost 10,100 killed and wounded, the Confederacy 9,700. When the list of missing was included, the total for both sides rose to 23,700, or nearly 22 percent of the armies engaged. The figures dispelled any dreams of a quick victory that remained on either side.

The South had lost an opportunity to stop Grant's drive into the western Confederacy, although the hard fighting had temporarily cost the Federals their momentum. But outnumbered and with a mangled army, it seemed doubtful that Beauregard could resume any offensive operations in the near future.

The change in command did not slow the hard-charging Confederates, but the Union army survived this bloody Sunday. The reason was largely stubborn resistance shown by a portion of Prentice's division in the center of the battle. Taking a strong position along a sunken road, Prentice's men fought so fiercely that the area came to be known as the "Hornet's Nest." Men fell by the score. A small pool of water nearby, thereafter called "Bloody Pond," offered some succor to the wounded. The Confederates massed sixty-two cannon in an attempt to break Prentice's line. But the men in blue held on until they were surrounded and forced to surrender. Prentice and some twenty-two hundred of his soldiers became prisoners, but they had given Grant time to bring up reinforcements, including troops from Buell's army, which arrived in time for the next day's fight. If Prentice had not slowed the Confederates, there might not have been a fight the next day.

As it was, the battle had raged for some thirteen hours when Beauregard finally ordered his men to halt and regroup. Earl Van Dorn's Arkansas army was expected anytime but had not yet arrived, and the Confederates had fought about as much as they could in one day. Shells from Union gunboats also made it difficult to push any closer to Pittsburg Landing.

31

Peach Orchard, Shiloh National Military Park, Tennessee

Shiloh Church (right) and Manse
George Cabin (below)

The Sunken Road (above) and the Bloody Pond (following pages), Shiloh

Grant's Last Line, Shiloh

Tennessee River, Pittsburg Landing, Shiloh

Attack on Fort Pulaski

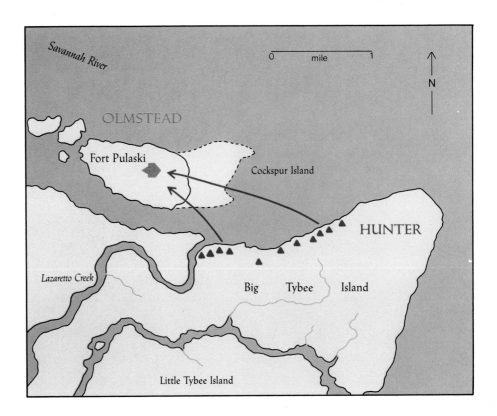

Fort Pulaski   GEORGIA

APRIL 10–11, 1862

FORT PULASKI LIES on Cockspur Island at the mouth of the Savannah River where the river empties into the Atlantic on the Georgia coast. When civil war broke out in 1861, the Confederacy occupied the fort to protect the nearby port city of Savannah. The structure rose above the surrounding marshy landscape some twenty-five feet above high tide. The fort was pentagon-shaped and had walls seven and a half feet thick. Although it had been designed for about 140 guns, Pulaski contained only 38 by the time the Union decided to attack in early 1862.

In an attempt to take Fort Pulaski, Federal commanders installed eleven batteries on the north shore of Tybee Island, just southeast of Cockspur. In order to encircle the fort as much as the marshes would allow, the Federals also placed a battery at Venus Point on James Island to the northwest of Cockspur. James Island forms the northeast bank of the Savannah River between the confluence of the Savannah and the Mud and Wright rivers. Directly across the Savannah's main channel from Venus Point, another battery was placed on the northwest point of Bird Island. In

a further effort to cut off the fort from communication with the mainland, two infantry companies and three pieces of artillery covered Lazaretto Creek due south of Pulaski.

Early on the morning of April 10, 1862, Union General David Hunter sent a representative under a flag of truce to demand the surrender of Fort Pulaski. The Confederate commander, Colonel Charles H. Olmstead, refused, declaring that his mission was to defend, not to surrender, the fort.

About 8:15 A.M., Federal batteries opened fire, and both sides exchanged a heavy barrage of artillery throughout the day. The large Union Parrott and James rifled cannon on Tybee Island soon began to chip away at the southeast face of Pulaski. By late evening, the Yankee cannoneers could see an ever-widening breach in the fort's wall. The Federal firing continued at a reduced rate through the night to discourage sorties by the Rebels against some of the more vulnerable Union batteries.

On the morning of April 11, the bombardment resumed in earnest. By midday two casemates on the southeast wall had been totally breached, and Federal shells had hit the fort's magazine.

The wide gap encouraged Hunter to organize a storming party of infantry. But by 2:00 P.M., Olmstead had had enough. The fort's thick walls had protected his men adequately, but his force of 385 was too small to withstand a direct assault, and with the wall hammered apart, he lacked the firepower to block a Yankee infantry attack. The colonel raised a white flag, and Union General Quincy Gillmore accepted his surrender.

The fort had received some 5,275 shells, including 3,500 from the big rifled pieces. The breach in the wall measured some thirty feet. Despite the storm of shells, casualties were practically nil. The Confederates had four seriously wounded, the Federals one killed.

The fall of Pulaski was another step in the Union's efforts to blockade Southern ports. As the war progressed, it became more and more apparent that the South did not have enough men to fight land battles and defend its coastline. Reduced access to the outside world weakened the Confederacy's chances of survival.

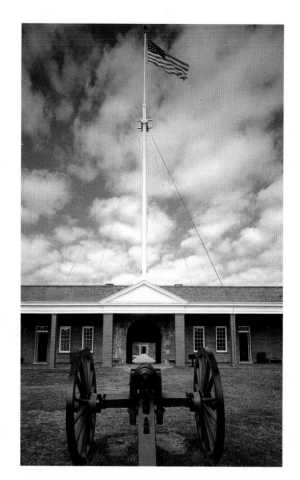

Entrance to Fort Pulaski and cannon (this page); reflection of fortification in moat (following pages)

South channel of the Savannah River, Fort Pulaski National Monument, Georgia

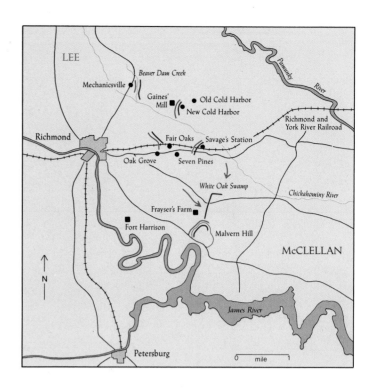

Seven Days   VIRGINIA

JUNE 25–JULY 1, 1862

IN THE AFTERMATH of First Manassas, General George McClellan replaced Irvin McDowell as commander of the Union Army of the Potomac and the retiring Winfield Scott as commander of all Federal armies. McClellan whipped the army into a polished outfit, but he also revealed his cautious nature as months dragged by and the army remained inactive.

Not until March 1862 did McClellan begin an offensive. He had decided to attack Richmond from the Atlantic seaboard by marching up the peninsula between the York and James Rivers east of the city. Once the plan had been made, McClellan continually delayed its implementation. He convinced himself that the Confederates had him thoroughly outnumbered, which was untrue, and he grew angry at President Abraham Lincoln for insisting that some of McClellan's force must remain behind to defend Washington. From March to June 1862, Stonewall Jackson's brilliant Shenandoah Valley campaign increased Lincoln's anxiety. Lincoln suspected that McClellan exaggerated Rebel strength. The president grew impatient and applied more pressure. Finally McClellan ordered his army aboard transports and sailed to the peninsula. Once he had disembarked his 100,000 men, the general continued to

move slowly, giving the Confederates time to concentrate to meet him.

On May 31, Joseph E. Johnston ordered the Confederate army to attack a part of McClellan's force at a place called Seven Pines (also known as Fair Oaks). For two days the Rebels of Generals James Longstreet and Gustavus Smith slugged it out with Federal forces of Generals Edwin Sumner, E. D. Keyes, and Stanley Heintzelman. During the action, Johnston received a severe wound, and on June 1, President Jefferson Davis gave his military adviser, Robert E. Lee, command of the army, which Lee promptly named the Army of Northern Virginia. Reinforcements were pulled in from all over Virginia. Lee's cavalry chief, J. E. B. Stuart, unnerved McClellan by executing a raid that completely encircled the huge Union army.

Having accumulated some eighty-five thousand men, Lee planned to begin his campaign against McClellan with an attack against General Fitz-John Porter's corps just north of the Chickahominy River, a major stream between the York and the James. Porter was isolated from the rest of the Union army, which lay south of the Chickahominy. Porter had apparently been left in this vulnerable position so that he could link up with any reinforcements Lincoln might send overland from Washington.

On Wednesday, June 25, while Lee finalized plans for his offensive, McClellan ordered an advance against the Confederate right. The ensuing Battle of Oak Grove never amounted to very much, as it had no effect on the positioning of the armies or on Lee's resolve to go ahead with his plans to hit Porter on the Union right.

On June 26, Confederate General A. P. Hill marched his corps towards Porter's position just east of Mechanicsville behind Beaver Dam Creek. Stonewall Jackson, who had been brought in from the Shenandoah, was to attack Porter's right flank while Hill made a frontal assault. Hill moved up and waited for Jackson. Hours passed with no sign of Stonewall. Late in the afternoon the impetuous Hill ordered an attack which was thrown back by Porter with heavy Rebel casualties.

After the Battle of Mechanicsville (also called Beaver Dam Creek or Ellerson's Mill), Porter decided to retreat to a formidable position east of the hamlet of Gaines' Mill. On June 27, Hill again attacked, this time with the support of Jackson and James Longstreet. Porter also received some reinforcements but not enough to hold his position. Under the cover of darkness, Porter managed to get his men across to the south bank of the Chickahominy,

Beaver Dam Creek, Richmond National Battlefield Park, Virginia

White Oak Swamp, Richmond

thereby ending the Battle of Gaines' Mill (also called the Battle of the Chickahominy or First Cold Harbor).

As a result of Porter's retreat, McClellan shifted his supply line from the railroad along the York River north of the Chickahominy to the James River south of his battle line. Lee's aggression had convinced McClellan that he was right about being outnumbered. McClellan forgot about taking Richmond and began worrying about getting his army off the peninsula before it was crushed.

Confederate pressure continued on June 28 as Lee's army followed Porter across the Chickahominy. Lee hoped to attack the Union eastern, or right, flank as McClellan pulled back toward the James. Delays made it necessary to scuttle the plan. On Sunday, June 29, Lee's advance was temporarily stopped by a tough Federal delaying action at Savage's Station.

On June 30, Lee tried to cut off McClellan's retreat at Frayser's Farm. The attack did not get under way until late in the evening when outnumbered Confederates surged into action. The battle raged well into the night. Hill supported Longstreet's men, who bore the brunt of the fight against four Union divisions. Enough units, including Jackson's whole corps, were in the area for the Confederates to have won the day. But none came up to help. Jackson, who had waged the successful Shenandoah campaign, had performed poorly from the very beginning of the Seven Days battles. He appeared to be suffering from severe fatigue and lacked his usual aggressiveness. The Federal divisions did retreat during the night, but a retreat had been intended anyway. Lee had lost thirty-three hundred men at the Battle of Frayser's Farm (also called White Oak Swamp) and had gained nothing.

On Tuesday, July 1, Lee made one last effort to smash McClellan. He ordered an attack against strong Union defenses at Malvern Hill, a prominent elevation near the James. Hill and Longstreet rested their men while the rest of the army attacked. With supporting fire from gunboats on the James, the well-entrenched Union army won a resounding victory. Lee had no choice but to allow McClellan to escape back to Washington. The Army of the Potomac left behind some sixteen thousand casualties.

Lee had lost nearly twenty thousand men, but Richmond had been saved and Lee and the Army of Northern Virginia would become legends. Lee's first successful campaign had not been picturesque. The victory reflected good fortune and revealed McClellan's incompetence. The Seven Days set the tone for future campaigns in Virginia. For another year, the Confederates would continue to win and the Union army would continue to suffer under poor leadership.

Cannon at Fort Harrison in Richmond National Military Park, Virginia (left); Chickahominy River (following pages)

49

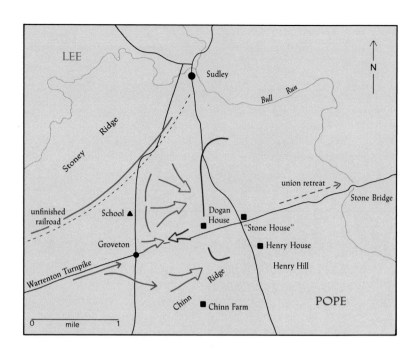

Second Manassas VIRGINIA

AUGUST 29–30, 1862

WHILE GEORGE MCCLELLAN retreated from the peninsula east of Richmond, President Abraham Lincoln decided to concentrate scattered Union forces in northern Virginia, which Robert E. Lee had chosen to ignore. Lincoln gave command of this newly created army to General John Pope, who had become something of a celebrity by engineering the capture of Island No. 10 on the Mississippi River, a victory highlighted by its occurrence on the day after the Confederate retreat from Shiloh.

Pope, a rather pompous braggart, instantly announced that he would soon take care of "Bobby" Lee. The general was a favorite of Northern radical Republicans and was quickly dubbed by Lee "the miscreant Pope." Personal feelings aside, however, Lee saw that he needed to deal with Pope's forty-five thousand troops before McClellan could return to Washington and merge the two Federal armies.

In early August, Lee therefore ordered Stonewall Jackson to march his corps toward Pope's position near Culpeper. Jackson won a battle on August 9, 1862, at Cedar Mountain against a portion of the Union Second and Third Corps. Pope had been bloodied but was not overly concerned. He knew he had Jackson outnumbered, and he did not think Lee would abandon Richmond

and bring the rest of the army to join Jackson. As usual, Lee did the unexpected. But Pope learned of Lee's intentions and retreated toward Washington to await McClellan. Lee then determined to draw Pope into battle as soon as possible.

While James Longstreet held Pope's attention along the Rapidan River, Jackson moved northwest to come in behind Pope's right flank. The maneuver kept Pope guessing as to what Lee had in mind. Jackson raided Union supply depots at Bristoe Station and at Manassas. Pope hesitated and finally decided to go after Jackson, who appeared to be retreating. Unsure where the Confederates were, Pope moved his men this way and that until late in the afternoon on Thursday, August 28, when Jackson intentionally revealed his position north of Groveton on the Warrenton Turnpike. As Lee had hoped, Pope attacked on August 29 without waiting for McClellan.

Pope hurled his army against Jackson's line along a ridge one hundred yards to the rear of an unfinished railroad bed. A. P. Hill's division received the main thrust of the Union assault, which almost gave Pope a victory before Lee arrived with James Longstreet's corps. During the early fighting, two Federal brigades mauled

Hill's left while four more under the command of Generals Joe Hooker and Jesse Reno charged the rest of Hill's men. At mid-afternoon, Hooker sent a fresh brigade into a gap in the Rebel line. Only desperate, determined resistance by the brigades of Maxcy Gregg and Ed Thomas saved Hill's division from destruction and Jackson's corps from defeat. The fighting waned late in the evening, but as night approached, Union General Phil Kearney led yet another charge at Hill's line. Many of the Confederates were out of ammunition, so they swung rifle butts and hurled barrages of rocks into the Federal ranks. Once more the line held. Fitz-John Porter moved to attack Jackson's right flank but ran into lead elements of Longstreet's corps, and the fighting ended for the night. Of all the bloody, desperate combats of the war, few struggles surpassed the first day of Second Manassas.

The morning of August 30 passed quietly. Pope finally convinced himself that Lee was retreating and ordered another mass attack against Jackson's line. The fighting was as bitter and desperate as the day before. The Federals charged bravely and, in the words of a Confederate officer, were "slaughtered . . . like hogs. I never saw the like of dead men in all my life." As

Battlefield, Manassas National Battlefield Park, Virginia (above) and Confederate fortifications at Manassas (left); Stone House, Manassas (following pages)

the final attack wave staggered and fell back, Pope ordered another advance. At this point, Longstreet sent his corps headlong into Pope's exposed left flank. Like a gray door swinging shut, Longstreet's line closed toward Jackson's front with Pope's army caught in between. Seizing the opportunity, Hill ordered his beleaguered division to charge. Union resistance crumbled, and Longstreet began extending his line along the south side of Warrenton Turnpike toward Henry house hill, a landmark of First Manassas. If Longstreet's tactics succeeded, Pope's main line of retreat would be cut off. But hard-fighting Union troops pushed back the Confederates and held the hill until nightfall. The Henry house, severely damaged the year before, was battered to the ground.

Pope had saved his army, but poor decisions had cost him some fourteen thousand men, counting missing and captured, during the Second Manassas campaign (called Second Bull Run in the North). Lee had lost ten thousand, a larger percentage than Pope, but once more Lee's aggressive generalship and his confident army had sent a poorly led Federal force scurrying back to Washington.

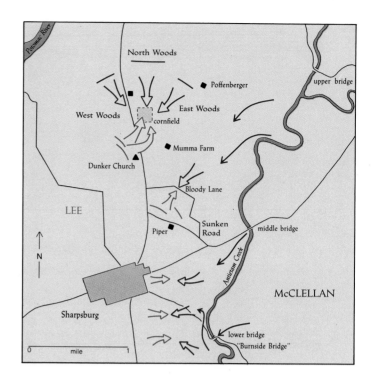

Antietam   MARYLAND

SEPTEMBER 17, 1862

THE CONFEDERATES had enjoyed a winning streak in Virginia, but the victories had created little more than a stalemate. The Army of the Potomac was just as much a threat as ever, especially if it ever received the leadership it deserved. Consequently Robert E. Lee and Jefferson Davis decided that an invasion of the North would be a risk worth taking. The fruits of a successful campaign might be increased support in the North for a negotiated peace, diplomatic recognition of the Confederacy by foreign nations, and recruits for the army in Maryland, where Confederate sympathies appeared strong.

On September 4, 1862, Lee's army of some fifty-five thousand men crossed the Potomac River near Leesburg, Virginia, into Maryland. Showing his disdain for George McClellan, Lee turned his army westward and split it into four groups. Three columns led by Stonewall Jackson moved toward the Federal arsenal at Harpers Ferry. Lee wanted the garrison there captured in order to secure his supply line into the Shenandoah Valley. While Jackson converged on his target, James Longstreet moved across South Mountain, a long ridge that ran northeast from the Potomac across western Maryland. On the western side of the mountain, Lee's

movements would be easier to screen from McClellan. (McClellan still commanded the Army of the Potomac, but Henry Halleck had taken over as commander of all Union armies. John Pope had been sent west to fight Indians.)

Unfortunately for Lee, a copy of his Orders No. 191 detailing his campaign plans fell into McClellan's hands. If McClellan acted quickly, he could take advantage of the isolated Rebel columns as he should already have done. But McClellan showed that Lee had been correct in thinking he could divide his army with the enemy at his back. McClellan procrastinated, and by the time two Union corps led by Generals Ambrose Burnside and William Franklin charged up South Mountain, Lee, who had learned of the lost order, had begun plugging Crampton's and Turner's gaps, the main passages across the mountain. The Battle of South Mountain thundered along the highlands throughout Sunday, September 14, as Lee struggled to buy time in which to concentrate his army.

The next day the Army of Northern Virginia, minus Jackson's corps, retreated back toward the Potomac. As the Rebels marched into Sharpsburg, Lee received word that Harpers Ferry had been captured and that Jackson's corps, not including A. P. Hill's division,

which was handling the details of surrender, was on the way to rejoin the army. Lee decided to make a stand behind Antietam Creek, an inconsiderable stream that ran northeast to southwest just east of Sharpsburg. Once more McClellan had an opportunity, for if he attacked at once, Lee's small force would have been overwhelmed. But once more McClellan hesitated, and by the time he was ready to give battle on September 17, Jackson had arrived. Still McClellan enjoyed nearly a two-to-one advantage, but as on the Peninsula, he also still believed that Lee had the numerical advantage. As a result another golden opportunity to end the war vanished.

The Battle of Antietam (called Sharpsburg in the South) opened on Lee's left flank north of Sharpsburg where Jackson had posted his men. Joe Hooker began the Federal attacks that would be conducted piecemeal from the Union right, shifting to the left as the day wore on. Because McClellan never brought his full army into battle at one time, Lee had the opportunity to move his men as needed.

During the morning hours from 6:00 to 9:00 A.M., Hooker, Sumner, and Joseph Mansfield hammered away at Jackson's divisions, led by Jubal Early, Lafayette McLaws, and John Bell

Wounded Confederates in makeshift tents of blankets and bayonets, near Antietam battlefield

Hood. The fighting spread over the Poffenberger, Miller, and Mumma farms, Miller's cornfield, the North, East, and West woods, and the Dunker Church. A New Yorker said of the struggle, "The fire and smoke, flashing of muskets and whizzing of bullets, yells of men, etc., were perfectly horrible." The battle ended in a stalemate, the best Lee could have hoped for.

The conflict now shifted to the center of the Confederate line. From 9:30 to 1:00 P.M., Daniel Harvey Hill's Rebels held a sunken road against the headlong assaults of William French's and Israel Richardson's divisions of Sumner's corps. The Federals had little cover, and Hill's men shot the first wave down as "grain falls before a reaper." The struggle along the sunken road was as hellish as any the war produced. Dead bodies filled the roadbed. A total of nearly five thousand men in blue and gray died, giving the road its name

Bloody Lane. McClellan could have won here if he had exploited a gap in the Confederate line caused by a mistaken order. But the attack that might have finished the Army of Northern Virginia never came.

The final phase of the battle lasted from 1:00 to 5:30 P.M. on the Confederate right. Ambrose Burnside advanced his corps toward a bridge across Antietam Creek. Despite the fact that he faced only a few hundred Georgians, Burnside moved slowly, taking much too long to seize the bridge that came to bear his name. Nevertheless, he almost crushed Lee's right. A. P. Hill's timely arrival from Harpers Ferry saved the army. Clad in his famous red flannel battle shirt, Hill rushed his men forward and stopped Burnside on the western slopes of the Antietam. This may have been the moment that Lee recalled when he lay near death several years later and murmured in delirium that Hill must

come up.

Lee had won a stalemate and had barely avoided a devastating defeat. But he refused to be driven from the field. He had lost 11,000 men in a battle which, including 12,500 Union casualties, had produced the greatest one-day bloodbath of the war. Yet Lee did not believe that McClellan would force the issue, and indeed the next day passed quietly. That evening Lee retreated back into Virginia.

The Confederate army had avoided catastrophe, but the campaign had failed. Marylanders did not flock to Lee's ranks, foreign recognition did not come, and Abraham Lincoln took the occasion to issue the Emancipation Proclamation, which changed the public perception of the war by shifting the emphasis from preservation of the Union to the liberation of Southern slaves. Such were the fruits of this first Confederate invasion of the North.

Sunken Road, Antietam National Battlefield (right) and Confederate dead on the Hagerstown pike, Antietam

Antietam National Battlefield, Maryland

Burnside Bridge, Antietam

Piper farm area, Antietam

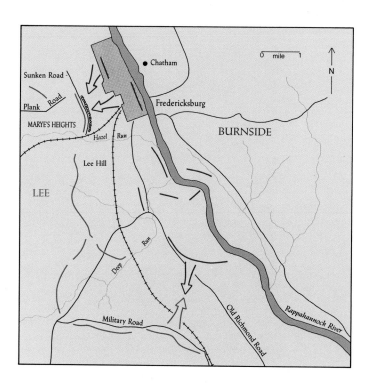

Fredericksburg VIRGINIA

DECEMBER 13, 1862

THE BATTLE OF ANTIETAM had been
fought. Weeks drifted by, and still
George McClellan did nothing. He had
waited while Robert E. Lee escaped from
Maryland, and now he showed no
willingness to take the offensive. A
disgusted Abraham Lincoln finally
dismissed McClellan and appointed
Ambrose Burnside as the new
commander of the Army of the
Potomac. Burnside had not performed
well at Antietam, and he sincerely did
not think himself capable of overall
command. But he had conducted a
successful campaign along the North
Carolina coast, and Lincoln would try
anyone who had succeeded anywhere.

Burnside reorganized his 120,000-man
army into three grand divisions,
commanded by William Franklin, Joe
Hooker, and Edwin Sumner. He then
proposed a frontal campaign against
Richmond. The army would move south
to the Rappahannock River, cross it,
take Fredericksburg, Virginia, and then
move straight for Richmond. To be
successful, Burnside needed to take
Fredericksburg before Lee occupied the
strategic heights that ran from the west
to the south of the city. As it happened,
delays in placing pontoon bridges
across the Rappahannock gave James
Longstreet's Confederate corps time to
march from Culpeper to those heights.

Before Burnside was ready to fight,
Stonewall Jackson's corps had arrived
from Winchester and had posted his
corps on Longstreet's right. While
Burnside waited, Lee had managed to
bring forward some eighty thousand
men to meet the Yankees.

Initially Burnside planned to throw
Franklin's entire grand division against
Jackson while Hooker and Sumner kept
Longstreet busy. This was a natural
strategy because Longstreet's men
occupied the almost impregnable
eminence known as Marye's Heights. A
sunken road ran along the base of the
heights, and a stone wall stood on the
side of the road facing the river. Between
the wall and the Rappahannock were a
canal and a drainage ditch. On the
Federal left, the approach from the river
to Jackson's position was more open
and flat and altogether much more
appealing.

On the morning of December 13,
Burnside hesitated and then ordered
Franklin to send only a part of his grand
division at Jackson while holding in
reserve enough men to protect the river
crossings. About 10:00 A.M. the sun
broke through a thick fog and revealed
fifty thousand Federal troops marching
majestically toward Jackson's
Confederates.

George Meade's division spearheaded

the Union assault that charged headlong
into the Rebel divisions of A. P. Hill and
Jubal Early. Meade temporarily broke
through Hill's line, but Jackson's well-
posted artillery drove the Yankees back.
The fighting raged for hours. Unless
Franklin brought up his reserves,
Jackson's line would obviously hold. But
Franklin was no more daring than
Burnside, and the Federals soon began
pulling back.

To relieve the pressure on Franklin,
Burnside decided to send Hooker and
Sumner in force against Longstreet.
This suicide mission fell to the divisions
of William French and Winfield
Hancock, who moved forward at about
noon. Artillery fire raked the advancing
blue columns as they left the protection
of buildings in Fredericksburg. The
lines closed and continued moving
forward in a display of bravery
comparable to any the war would
produce. From behind the stone wall
came a sheet of flaming musketry.
Union soldiers fell by the hundreds.
Still the line advanced, to within a
hundred yards, then to seventy-five. At
about sixty yards, the attack finally
broke.

French had lost about a third of his
division. Now Hancock's men took
their turn at the front as the Rebel
fire continued to gain in intensity.

Fredericksburg Battlefield of Fredericksburg and Spotsylvania Court House National Military Park, Virginia, viewed from Chatham, Virginia

Confederate soldiers liked the safety of the stone wall. More and more of them crowded along its length until they stood as much as four lines deep. One line fired and moved to the rear. Then the next line came up, creating a "cycle of fire that was more than four times the normal rate." For what it was worth, Hancock's men got a few yards closer than French's, but they fell just as thickly on ground that was now blanketed with blue-coated corpses. The two divisions had lost thirty-two hundred men. Meanwhile, Oliver O. Howard's division tried to flank the wall on the right, but Confederate fire forced his men back toward the center. Howard lost nine hundred men and gained nothing.

The assaults kept coming. Burnside grew more and more desperate. Hooker tried to dissuade him, but many more men died before darkness mercifully halted the slaughter. By the time it ended, Burnside had sent sixty-five hundred soldiers to their deaths. During the cold December night, many wounded died of exposure. Poorly clad Confederates went out between the lines and stripped the well-clothed Union dead.

The next day Burnside wanted to renew the battle, but subordinates talked him out of it. He had suffered more than twelve thousand casualties while inflicting only four thousand on the enemy. Lincoln was astounded at the news and worried about the political impact of the disaster. The demoralized Army of the Potomac withdrew across the river. A few weeks later, Burnside tried once more to cross the Rappahannock. Severe weather turned the operation into the infamous "mud march" and thwarted Burnside's plans. Soldiers must have wondered how victory at Antietam could so quickly have been transformed into nightmare at Fredericksburg. For Robert E. Lee's Army of Northern Virginia, the battle spelled redemption and offered hope of more successes in the new year of 1863.

The stone wall on the Sunken Road
at Fredericksburg during the war
(left) and today (below)

Stones River, Stones River National Battlefield, Tennessee

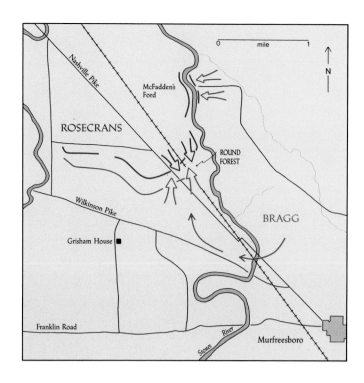

Stones River TENNESSEE

DECEMBER 31, 1862–JANUARY 2, 1863

AFTER SHILOH, P. G. T. Beauregard led his Confederate army back to Corinth, but overwhelming Union numbers soon forced a retreat to Tupelo. On June 27, 1862, Braxton Bragg replaced Beauregard after the Louisianan fell into disfavor with Jefferson Davis. A solid soldier but also a martinet who gave his men little inspiration, Bragg set about restoring the battered army back to fighting shape. By August, Bragg felt he was ready, and he ordered an advance into Middle Tennessee to draw Union general Don Carlos Buell's army away from Chattanooga, a valuable Confederate supply center. Bragg's campaign ultimately extended into Kentucky, where on October 8 he defeated Buell at Perryville. Here Bragg demonstrated a weakness that was fatal in a man charged with overall command. After winning a battle, he retreated. He simply lacked the special fire and tenacity that winning generals must have.

Bragg led his army back into Tennessee and established a camp at Murfreesboro, some twenty miles southeast of Nashville. Buell moved back to Nashville, where he was soon relieved of command because of his lackluster performance in Kentucky. General William Rosecrans, a worthy officer, if not a brilliant one, replaced Buell.

Rosecrans took his time in preparing to advance against Bragg—so much time, in fact, that official Washington threatened to remove him from command before he ever fought a battle. Not until Friday, December 26, 1862, did Rosecrans's forty-five-thousand-man Army of the Cumberland begin moving in three columns toward Murfreesboro. A young Confederate cavalry general, Joe Wheeler, brilliantly delayed the Federal march, giving Bragg time to position his troops and plan for the coming fight. On Monday, December 29, Rosecrans's lead elements finally reached the vicinity of Stones River, a small, fordable stream flowing from north to south on the west side of Murfreesboro.

Bragg deployed his thirty-eight thousand troops to the west and northwest of Stones River, with his right flank extending across the river to the east. The armies jockeyed for position throughout Tuesday, December 30. That night one of the most poignant events of the war developed along the cold Tennessee hillsides. Men of the North and the South, many no doubt sensing that they had enjoyed their last Christmas, joined together in singing the haunting strains of "Home Sweet Home."

The battle began the next morning at daybreak. As at First Manassas, each general planned to attack the other's flank, this time targeting the right wings. Bragg ordered his attack at dawn, whereas Rosecrans had scheduled his assault at 7:00 A.M. The Confederates moved out on time, and the corps of William Hardee and Leonidas Polk thundered into the unsuspecting camps of Rosecrans's right flank, held by General Alexander McCook's troops.

The Federals fought remarkably well under the circumstances, but the momentum of the Rebel attack was overwhelming. Facing certain death or capture, Union regiments quickly retreated. Among the cedar thickets that covered a large portion of the battlefield, a young general named Phil Sheridan distinguished himself by leading the fiercest resistance displayed by any of McCook's officers. But Sheridan's men too were soon forced back by the Rebel tide.

Noon came and went, and Bragg's attack was going exactly as planned. Rosecrans's right had been pushed back so far that it was now at a right angle to the position that McCook had held when the fighting started. The Union line reached a sharp point around the Nashville & Chattanooga Railroad

Stones River National Battlefield

where the hammered right wing connected with the relatively unbloodied left. Rosecrans put every man he could spare into this salient in order to stabilize his front. The salient area would be dubbed the Round Forest in battle reports, but soldiers who fought there called it "Hell's Half-Acre."

The battle raged on into the afternoon until Bragg finally ordered John C. Breckinridge to send reinforcements from across the river where he held the Confederate right wing. When the brigades arrived, they attacked piecemeal rather than en masse, thereby reducing the firepower that might have won the battle. As it was, night came, the fighting ended, and Rosecrans's line remained firm.

The Federals had taken a beating. Bragg thought that Rosecrans would surely retreat. In fact Rosecrans thought a lot about retreating. Instead he decided to spend the evening reorganizing and consolidating his lines. To do so he had to abandon the Round Forest to the Rebels.

Thursday came and went, and Bragg did nothing. The only movement on this quiet New Year's Day involved the Federal occupation of a ridge on the west bank of Stones River, directly opposite Breckinridge's position. It proved to be a profound move on Rosecrans's part.

The next day, January 2, Bragg decided to try an artillery crossfire to drive the Federals from the field. To carry out the plan, he needed the very ridge the Yankees had taken over. Breckinridge received orders to take the position, orders to which he strenuously objected. He considered the ridge impregnable, but Bragg prevailed. At 4:00 P.M. the Confederates advanced. The attack on the east side of the river went well, but when the Rebels got within range of the west bank, fifty-eight Union cannon brought the offensive to a bloody halt.

Bragg had had enough. His men had fought hard and had gained much, but he had lost his nerve. He convinced himself that Rosecrans would soon be reinforced. Consequently the Confederate army retreated on January 3. Bragg had inflicted thirteen thousand casualties while losing ten thousand men. But as in Kentucky, he had turned his back on a probable victory. At Stones River (also called the Battle of Murfreesboro), the fortunes of the western Confederacy continued to slide downhill.

Site of Fight for the Cedars, Stones River

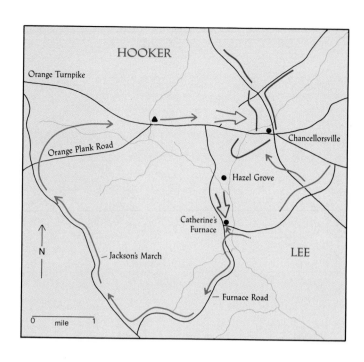

Chancellorsville VIRGINIA

MAY 1–4, 1863

THE ARMY OF THE POTOMAC marched into its first campaign of 1863 with another new commander, Joe Hooker. Fighting Joe instilled new life into the army with his positive attitude and, more important, by granting his men winter furloughs. With reinforcements and new recruits, Hooker had available for his first campaign some 135,000 troops, more than twice as many as Robert E. Lee had encamped at Fredericksburg.

Hooker set his massive army in motion on April 27. Three of seven corps marched to the west, where they would cross the Rapidan and Rappahannock rivers, turn east, and close in on Lee's rear. Two corps led by General John Sedgwick crossed the Rappahannock below Fredericksburg to draw Lee's attention in that direction. Two corps stayed behind in reserve to guard river fords and ultimately to join the three corps' flanking movement to the west.

Robert E. Lee had every reason to run from the fight that awaited him. He had earlier sent James Longstreet and two divisions into southeastern Virginia and the North Carolina coastal area to defend supply lines and to ship food to the main army. In the absence of these divisions, Lee had only sixty thousand men to face Hooker's two-front

Union artillery regulars before the Battle of Chancellorsville

offensive.

Apparently Lee never considered retreating. When he learned on April 2 that part of the Federal army was moving toward his left flank and rear, Lee sent first one division, then another, and finally three more under Stonewall Jackson to confront Hooker flanking force. Lee's caution in dispatching divisions did not reflect hesitancy. He merely wanted to be sur that the flank attack was indeed Hooker's main attack. Jubal Early's division stayed in Fredericksburg to confront Sedgwick while the rest of th Confederate army concentrated to the west.

Lee's lead divisions under Richard Anderson and Lafayette McLaws began entrenching when they met Hooker's vanguard near Chancellorsville, which was not a town but merely the area where the Chancellor house stood at a crossroads some ten miles west of Fredericksburg. When Jackson reached the Confederate line on May 1, he ordered an attack. If Sedgwick attacked and defeated Early at Fredericksburg, the Army of Northern Virginia would be caught in a vise. Entrenching took time that the Rebels did not have. Lee rode up and approved Jackson's order. The gray lines surged forward.

The Confederate charge caught the

Army of the Potomac by surprise. Hooker thought most of Lee's army was still in Fredericksburg. The Federal front reeled as Rebels came thundering down the Orange Turnpike and Orange Plank roads. Within a short time, Yankees east of Chancellorsville were in full retreat. The Union lines gave way so easily that Lee momentarily suspected his army of being lured into a trap.

As night fell on May 1, most of Hooker's main attack force was west of Chancellorsville, deployed on the Orange Turnpike and facing south as a result of the afternoon's fighting that had seen the Confederates push Hooker's right flank north of the Orange Plank road. Winfield Hancock's corps stretched east of Chancellorsville for a short distance on Hooker's left and then bent at a sharp angle to the north. Lee's initiative had in effect forced Hooker from a north-to-south front to a west-to-east-to-north disposition.

During the night Lee and Jackson met where Furnace Road crossed the Orange Plank Road. They concocted a plan that was even more audacious than Lee's earlier strategy. The army would divide again. Jackson would march his three divisions southwest down the Furnace Road, turn right onto the Brock Road, move northwest to the Orange Turnpike, wheel to the right and smash into the exposed Union right flank. Meanwhile, Lee with two divisions, fewer than twenty thousand men, would hold the present front against many times that number of Federals.

Jackson's march got under way early the next morning and took most of the daylight hours of May 2. Hooker made Lee's job easier by doing almost nothing that day. Clearly the surprise Confederate attack of May 1 had shaken the Union commander. To make matters worse, during the light action of May 2, a cannon shot hit pillars of the house being used as headquarters. A pillar fragment struck Hooker in the head, leaving him in a daze for several hours. The only significant thing he did was to order Sedgwick to send some men to Chancellorsville, a move that eased the pressure on Early at Fredericksburg. Fighting Joe seemed interested more in defending than in fighting.

All day Jackson's inexorable march creeped closer to its objective. By 5:15 p.m. his division was ready to go

Hazel Grove, Chancellorsville Battlefield of Fredericksburg and Spotsylvania Court House National Military Park, Virginia

forward. The charge swept Oliver O. Howard's Eleventh Corps away like a hurricane. The flank attack succeeded brilliantly, but the Confederacy paid a high price. After driving the Federals back for several hundred yards, Jackson fell severely wounded as he reconnoitered the front lines. In the dark, he had been shot accidentally by his own men. Eight days later he died. The Army of Northern Virginia never quite recovered. Still, Hooker had been beaten. Fighting continued, but by noon on May 3, the Union army was headed back toward Washington.

Jackson's charge gave Lee the opportunity to take care of the Sedgwick threat in his rear. At dawn on May 3, Sedgwick drove Early out of Fredericksburg and advanced westward to Salem Church, where Lafayette McLaw's division lay in his path.

Hooker thought only of escape after the destruction of his right flank; so Lee sent reinforcements to McLaws. On May 4, Sedgwick fell back and joined the rest of the Federal army in retreat.

Once more a huge Union army had been driven from the field, its numbers and fighting ability wasted by a weak commanding general. Hooker had lost sixteen thousand men to Lee's twelve thousand, but an aggressive officer with the numerical superiority Hooker enjoyed would have given a much better account of himself and would have kept on fighting regardless of casualties. Hooker's inadequacies did not detract from Lee's performance. Lee had indeed fought his greatest battle, but he had lost Stonewall Jackson. And he knew that, if Lincoln ever gave the Army of the Potomac a worthy commander, the Confederacy would be in trouble.

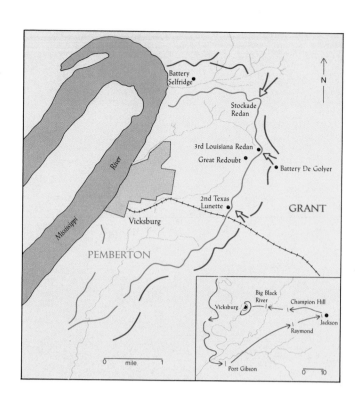

Vicksburg   MISSISSIPPI

MAY 19–JULY 4, 1863

BETWEEN THE CONFEDERATE evacuation of Corinth in the summer of 1862 and the coming of spring in 1863, the war on the western front had been fought to something of a draw. In September and October 1862, battles at Iuka and Corinth, Mississippi, had consolidated Union control of the northern part of the state. U. S. Grant turned his attention to Vicksburg, a heavily fortified town in west central Mississippi that was situated on high bluffs on the eastern bank of the Mississippi River.

In December, Grant embarked on a two-front campaign. He would lead a land force southward from northwest Mississippi while William T. Sherman took troops by boat down the Mississippi. Grant's part in the campaign was cancelled when Confederate cavalry made a devastating raid on his supply base at Holly Springs. Meanwhile, Sherman landed north of Vicksburg, waited in vain for Grant, decided to attack anyway, and was severely repulsed at the Battle of Chickasaw Bluffs on December 29.

Grant spent the early months of 1863 trying other plans to take Vicksburg. Attempts to flank the city from the north and the south by various water routes failed, as did an effort to divert the Mississippi away from Vicksburg by digging a canal across a narrow neck of land on the other side of the river. Finally in March 1863, Grant launched a plan that succeeded.

Two Union corps under Generals John McClernand and James McPherson marched southward down the west bank of the Mississippi. Grant then directed Admiral David Porter to run his fleet past the gauntlet of Confederate batteries along the Vicksburg waterfront. Porter was successful and lost only one boat during the operation. Farther downriver, Porter also managed to pass strong Confederate batteries posted near the town of Grand Gulf.

To keep Confederate commander John C. Pemberton guessing, Grant left Sherman's corps near Vicksburg to feint at the Chickasaw Bayou area. Meanwhile, Benjamin Grierson's cavalry embarked on a raid from northeast to southwest Mississippi. With a large portion of his cavalry transferred to the Army of Tennessee, Pemberton had a nightmarish time trying to keep track of all the Federal activity.

By the time Pemberton realized that Grant intended to flank Vicksburg on the south, the Union army had been transferred to the east side of the river by Porter's boats and was streaming toward the town of Port Gibson. Grant planned to veer northeast toward the state capital at Jackson and then move west to Vicksburg. Pemberton realized that he stood the best chance of stopping Grant by beating him near the river.

On May 1, Confederate forces led by General John Bowen, an aggressive and brilliant field commander, met Grant's army a few miles west of Port Gibson. Though outnumbered nearly three to one, Bowen's eight thousand fought hard and, aided by the tangled terrain of steep bluffs blanketed with thick undergrowth, held Grant in check nearly all day. But Pemberton could not get enough reinforcements to the battle in time, and Bowen retreated toward Vicksburg. Grant's army moved on toward Jackson.

On May 12, a portion of McPherson's corps defeated a small Rebel force near Raymond. On May 14, McPherson and Sherman, whose corps had rejoined the main army, defeated a makeshift Confederate army led by Joseph E. Johnston at Jackson. Johnston had been sent to Mississippi to assume overall command, but Pemberton still reported directly to Jefferson Davis. Despite Johnston's decision to abandon Vicksburg, Pemberton decided to obey Davis's dictum that the city must never

Navy monument, Vicksburg National Military Park, Vicksburg

be given up. Johnston's heart was never in the campaign, he was not fond of offensive warfare, and all in all, Davis's decision to send Johnston to Mississippi only made things worse for Pemberton and easier for Grant.

After running Johnston out of Jackson, Grant moved his thirty-two thousand troops toward Vicksburg. Pemberton concentrated twenty-three thousand troops (not counting Johnston's men, who were north of Jackson near Canton) to confront Grant east of the Big Black River. Pemberton had decided to try to join Johnston but ran into Grant's army first and was defeated at the Battle of Champion Hill on May 16. Pemberton's army fought well, but the Pennsylvania-born

Confederate general had uncooperative officers who constantly obstructed his efforts to shift troops during the fighting. One of those officers was William Wing Loring, who escaped with his division and joined Johnston. The demoralized Confederates retreated from Champion Hill, and the rear guard of the army was defeated again at the Big Black River crossing. But Pemberton did maneuver his army back inside the considerable Vicksburg defenses.

Pemberton's army had been kicked around, but it could still fight, as Grant soon learned. The Federal army drew up around Vicksburg and on May 19 assaulted the Rebel lines. On the Confederate right and center, the

Yankees made some progress but came nowhere near penetrating enemy lines. On the left, Sherman threw his corps against that portion of Pemberton's line known as Stockade Redan. Bowen's crack infantry shredded Sherman's lines. Many of the Federals hugged the ground until darkness made it possible to retreat safely. Grant lost almost one thousand men during the fighting, but he determined to try again.

On May 22, Sherman again tested the Confederate left with the same results. McPherson rushed toward the center and took a beating in front of the Third Louisiana Redan and the Great Redoubt. On the Union left, McClernand met with limited success in his assault on the Second Texas

THE SHIRLEY HOUSE

SHIRLEY HOUSE IN 1863

The house before you is the only surviving wartime structure in the park. On May 26th Union forces started digging an approach to the 3rd Louisiana Redan from near here. Several days later, the Confederates opened fire on the workers with a cannon mounted in the redan. The Yankees countered with artillery of the "White House Battery," named after this house.

Shirley House, Vicksburg, today (top) and slope in front of Shirley House, with burrows where Confederate men lived as they prepared for Union troops

Lunette, but he too was forced back.

Two assaults having failed, Grant decided to besiege the city. Weeks passed, and reinforcements poured into the Federal lines. Johnston gathered a force of some thirty-five thousand to help break the siege, but he procrastinated until it was too late. Pemberton's supplies dwindled, and his army and the citizens of Vicksburg were subjected to unrelenting shelling from artillery and gunboats.

With conditions worsening, and Johnston apparently having no intention of mounting a rescue operation, Pemberton decided he must surrender. Convinced that Grant would give him good terms, Pemberton chose to give up the fight on July 4. Pemberton knew he would be ostracized in the South for surrendering on a Federal holiday, but he did get his way otherwise when Grant agreed to parole the Confederates rather than sending them to Northern prison camps. Many of the captured Rebels would soon be fighting for the South again.

The fall of Vicksburg left the Trans-Mississippi Confederacy isolated, but it had been politically isolated for some time anyway. The real blow to the Confederacy was the loss of free access to the Mississippi, a vital supply artery. Grant's victory bolstered his stock and set him on the road to greater fame. Pemberton felt disgraced by the loss. How would he have felt if he had known that, the day before he surrendered, his boyhood friend George Meade had won the greatest battle of the war in Pennsylvania?

Cavalryman, Wisconsin monument (above) and Mississippi monument (right), Vicksburg

Mississippi River, viewed from Battery Selfridge, Vicksburg National Military Park, Mississippi

Confederate Brigadier General Lloyd Tilghman statue, Vicksburg

Frieze on Missouri monument, Vicksburg

Vicksburg National Military Park, Mississippi

Michigan monument, Vicksburg

Mississippi statue, Seminary Ridge, Gettysburg National Military Park, Pennsylvania

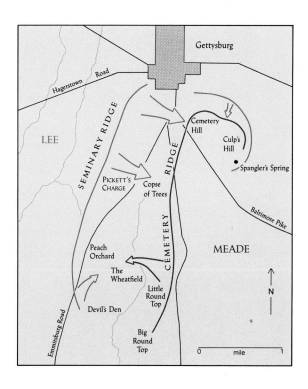

Gettysburg PENNSYLVANIA

July 1–3, 1863

In early June 1863, Robert E. Lee marched the Army of Northern Virginia toward Maryland and his ultimate destination, Pennsylvania. Lee and Jefferson Davis had decided to invade the North again for the same reasons that they had had in 1862. The campaign might also keep reinforcements from U. S. Grant at Vicksburg. After Stonewall Jackson's death, Lee had reorganized his army into three corps commanded by Richard Ewell, A. P. Hill, and James Longstreet. Ewell led the march north, followed by Longstreet and Hill.

Joe Hooker wanted to capture Fredericksburg and Richmond while Lee was out of the way, but official Washington refused him permission. Abraham Lincoln thought Lee's army a more important target, and anyway he wanted Washington protected. So Hooker and the Army of the Potomac shadowed the invading Rebels, always keeping between the enemy and the capital.

Dick Ewell's long gray line moved on into Pennsylvania and occupied Chambersburg on June 24. Ewell then moved to the northeast into Carlisle and to the outskirts of Harrisburg, the state capital. Meanwhile, Hill and Longstreet came into Chambersburg, turned east, and marched through

Gettysburg and York and on to Wrightsville.

During all this time, Lee did not know what Hooker was doing. J. E. B. Stuart had taken his cavalry on a reconnaissance ride around the Union army and had not returned. Without his cavalry, Lee was in the dark. He did not know that Hooker had been replaced by George Meade, a tough, veteran soldier who was much more able than his predecessors. Meade moved his army quickly across the Potomac on June 26 and marched north through Frederick, Maryland, toward Harrisburg. If he arrived while Lee's army was divided, the Confederates would be in serious trouble. Lee learned of the threat on June 28 and sent orders for his corps commanders to concentrate west of Gettysburg at Cashtown. Here he would fight or feint toward Washington to pull Meade eastward away from the Confederate supply line.

Meade planned to concentrate his army southeast of Gettysburg to guard against possible Rebel advances toward Baltimore and Washington. On June 30, part of his cavalry rode into Gettysburg, seeking information on the Rebels, and encountered a Confederate brigade looking for shoes. The Confederates chose to retire rather than fight, but the contact drew both armies toward

Gettysburg. While there would have been a collision sooner or later, the coming battle had found its site quite by accident.

During the early morning hours of Wednesday, July 1, Henry Heth's division of A. P. Hill's corps marched down the Chambersburg Pike toward Gettysburg. Heth intended to find out just how many Federals were in the town. On the previous night, brigades of Meade's First Cavalry Division, led by John Buford, had been deployed west and north of Gettysburg to keep an eye on Confederate activity and to protect the army's left flank. Buford's horsemen and Heth's infantry exchanged the opening shots of the battle.

Though they were outnumbered, the Yankee cavalry fought stubbornly, giving Meade time to bring up his infantry to occupy a strategic ridge south of Gettysburg. Federals from General John Reynold's corps hurried forward to support Buford. Reynold's troops drove Heth back, but Reynolds was shot dead and was replaced temporarily by Abner Doubleday, who would eventually become famous as the inventor of the game of baseball. More Union infantry came up, including Oliver Howard's corps, which had been mauled at Chancellorsville. Additional Confederate divisions from the corps of

Gouveneur Kemble Warren statue, Little Round Top, Gettysburg

Hill and Ewell marched to the scene from Carlisle and Harrisburg. The weight of the Rebel concentration broke the Union left, which fell back to Cemetery Ridge, valuable ground that Buford's hard fighting had saved for Meade. The Confederate right, anchored by Hill with Ewell on the left, advanced and occupied Seminary Ridge, which lay parallel to Cemetery Ridge and to the west.

On the Confederate left, the opposing armies struggled throughout the day in what proved to be the decisive action at Gettysburg. Jubal Early's division of Ewell's corps drove in Meade's right through Gettysburg to Cemetery Hill, which anchored the north end of Cemetery Ridge. Lee ordered Ewell to press forward, take the hill, and force Meade to evacuate the ridge. But Early's division procrastinated, Ewell did nothing, and Meade rushed Winfield Hancock forward to firm up Federal lines in the area. Ewell never made the attack, and Lee lost his best chance to break the Union line on Cemetery Ridge. Lee must have wondered what the outcome might have been if Stonewall Jackson had been present.

On July 2, Lee decided to attack Meade's flanks. The job would be difficult, for the Union line had stabilized into a fishhook. The shaft of the hook ran from south to north along Cemetery Ridge. At the north end, the line curved around to the right along Cemetery Hill and Culp's Hill. At the southern end lay two prominent, sharply defined eminences, Big Round Top and Little Round Top. Meade had been slow to occupy the round tops, and his left was vulnerable to attack there.

Neither Ewell nor Longstreet, whose corps now held the Confederate right, supported Lee's plan. Each thought Meade's line too strong to be assaulted, and Longstreet tried to convince Lee that the army should maneuver Meade off the ridge and find more suitable terrain to fight. Lee was adamant, however, and ordered both generals to attack. Longstreet would make the main thrust, while Ewell pinned down the Yankee right flank.

Planning Longstreet's offensive took hours, and when his corps finally got under way, the march was delayed by terrain which forced much marching and countermarching to shield his route from the Federals. At about 4:30 P.M., he attacked. The fighting raged into the night over areas that have become

Confederate campsite, Gettysburg

well known in Civil War lore: the Wheatfield, Devil's Den, Peach Orchard, and the two round tops. Federal troops had occupied the round tops in time to repulse Longstreet's attack and to save Meade's flank. But Longstreet did take some ground, and though Meade's line held, his men did take quite a pounding. On the other end of the battle line, Ewell's troops moved slowly, briefly occupied Culp's Hill, and then fell back under the weight of Federal reinforcements.

Having failed on the flanks, Lee decided on July 3 to charge Meade's center. Given the strength of the Union line, the plan was foolish, but Lee had developed supreme confidence in his men to do the impossible. Over Longstreet's strong objections, Lee ordered General George Pickett's division of Longstreet's corps plus elements from A. P. Hill's three divisions, some fifteen thousand men, to make the attack. At 3:00 P.M., the gray ranks marched forward as if on parade into a storm of artillery and

musketry. Scores fell. The ranks closed up and kept coming. A few Rebels actually made it to the Federal line near a grove of trees. The spot has been called the "high-water mark of the Confederacy," but it was more correctly the high-water mark of Lee's army. The survivors of the charge moved sullenly back down the ridge, leaving behind some seven thousand killed and wounded.

The battle was over; Lee knew he must retreat. In three days he had lost 28,000 of his 75,000 men. Meade had lost 23,000, but reinforcements had continued to filter in, and by the second day of the battle he had over 100,000 men. As at Antietam, Lee hesitated before retreating, and as at Antietam, he retreated unharried by the enemy.

Gettysburg was a turning point. Lee never again grasped the offensive initiative that had come to symbolize his generalship. But the change resulted more from effective Union generalship than from the battle lost in Pennsylvania.

Cemetery Hill, Gettysburg

The Wheatfield, Gettysburg

Devil's den (above) and Little Round Top (right)

Cemetery Hill, Gettysburg

Robert E. Lee Statue, Virginia monument, Gettysburg

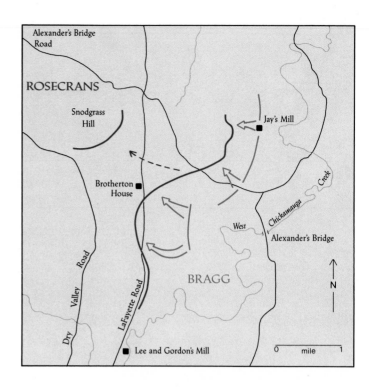

Chickamauga GEORGIA

September 19–20, 1863

BRAXTON BRAGG RETREATED to
Tullahoma, Tennessee, after giving up
the field at Stones River. For several
months, Bragg remained inactive, as did
William Rosecrans at Murfreesboro. In
late June 1863, Rosecrans finally set
his army in motion toward Bragg.
Rosecran's objectives included the
capture of Chattanooga, a Rebel supply
and rail center, and the placing of
enough pressure on Bragg to keep the
Confederacy from shifting troops of the
Army of Tennessee to assist John C.
Pemberton at Vicksburg.

Bragg retreated before Rosecrans's
offensive, trying to stay between the
enemy and Chattanooga. Rosecrans
conducted a campaign of maneuver,
continually wheeling toward Bragg's left
and gradually forcing the Confederates
into Chattanooga. Rosecrans's next step
was to cut off the city's southern supply
lines and force Bragg to surrender.

Wary of being trapped, Bragg
withdrew from Chattanooga on
September 9 and moved southward to
contemplate his next move. Rosecrans
occupied the city and then, mistaking
Bragg's retreat for an attempted escape
toward Atlanta, split his army into
three columns which moved toward
mountain passes southwest of
Chattanooga. Using mountains as a
screen, Rosecrans hoped that one or

more of his columns could move in
front of Bragg and cut off the Rebel
retreat.

Rosecran's deployments presented
Bragg with an opportunity to strike the
isolated Federal columns. With his
army spread along the east bank of
Chickamauga Creek a few miles south
of Chattanooga, Bragg watched and
waited for several days. He learned the
location of the two Yankee columns
nearest him, one led by John Crittenden
just below Chattanooga and another
commanded by George Thomas several
miles south of Crittenden. The third
column, that of Alexander McCook, had
drifted so far south that Bragg's cavalry
did not spot it for several more days.
Bragg attempted to take the offensive
against Rosecrans's divided troops, but
his plans were thwarted by a poor
relationship with most of his generals.
Orders were poorly communicated and
executed, and in the end practically
nothing was accomplished.

On September 18, Bragg finally got
his right wing under way in an assault
on Crittenden. But by then McCook had
arrived from the south, and the entire
Army of the Cumberland was forming
at Bragg's front. Bragg had a trump card,
however—reinforcements from the
Army of Northern Virginia. James
Longstreet brought his corps by rail

through the Carolinas and Atlanta to
reach the battlefield. On September
17–19, Longstreet's men filtered in on
the left of Bragg's line.

The action on the eighteenth left
Bragg in good shape to carry out his
plan to turn Rosecrans's left and drive
the Federals away from Chattanooga.
Bragg's right managed to drive across
Chickamauga Creek, flank Crittenden's
left, and bend it back to the south. Bragg
was now set for the coming fight. Until
all Longstreet's men came on the scene,
the Confederate battle line would
consist, from north to south, of corps
belonging to Leonidas Polk, W. H. T.
Walker, and Simon Buckner. Nathan
Bedford Forrest's cavalry patrolled the
right flank and Joe Wheeler's horsemen
the left.

During the night, Rosecrans
strengthened his position by shifting
George Thomas's corps to the left.
Crittenden now held the center and
McCook the right.

On Saturday, September 19, at 7:30
A.M., the battle opened at Jay's Mill
on the Union left. Both Bragg and
Rosecrans fed troops into the north end
of the battle line, and the area became
so crowded that the sheer force of
numbers extended the fight southward.
Neither side made much headway. A. P.
Stewart's division of Buckner's corps

Brotherton Cabin, Chickamauga and Chattanooga National Military Park, Georgia

Freize, at Wilder Tower, Chickamauga

dented and then defeated H. P. Van Cleve's division of Crittenden's corps, but Stewart's men were in turn forced to retire in the face of Federal artillery and infantry reinforcements. Pat Cleburne's division of Hill's corps fell back after running into a wall of fire on George Thomas's left. In this manner the fighting ebbed and flowed up and down the line. By nightfall, the heavily fortified Union left still held firm in advance of the rest of Rosecrans's line, which now lay west of the Lafayette Road.

Longstreet arrived that night, and Bragg decided to divide his army into two wings. Longstreet would command the left, comprising the corps of Buckner and John Bell Hood; Polk would command the right, consisting of his corps and those of D. H. Hill and

Walker. The changes did not alter Bragg's strategy. When the battle resumed on Sunday, Polk would continue to push Rosecrans's left, while Longstreet put pressure on the rest of the Federal line.

Rosecrans was also busy during the night. He pulled back and solidified his front by shortening it and shifting more men to the left. When Polk's assault, after much delay, got under way at 10:00 A.M. the next morning, the Confederates found log breastworks and heavy Federal fire awaiting them.

D. H. Hill's corps had been designated to lead the attack, but Hill was angry at being placed under Polk's command. So Hill sulked and delayed. When his attack finally came, it was poorly executed. Instead of trying to turn Thomas's left, Hill's division drove

straight ahead and got nowhere.

While Polk's wing struggled, Longstreet had remarkably good fortune. Erroneously informed that a gap existed near the center of his line, Rosecrans ordered a division to shift and cover the schism. The order created a gap rather than closing one, and Longstreet poured five divisions into the breach. Rosecrans's center and right disintegrated, and the survivors rolled back to the north. A Confederate described Longstreet's charge as "short and bloody" with "no halting."

Bragg did nothing to take advantage of the breakthrough. A general Confederate assault might have destroyed the Federal army, but the assault never came. With the Federal force left intact, George Thomas managed to rally a strong defense against Longstreet at an eminence called Snodgrass Hill. Thomas's action earned him the sobriquet "Rock of Chickamauga." His line held until 5:30, when the Federals withdrew to Chattanooga.

Bragg's victory might be called the true high-water mark of the Confederacy. An aggressive pursuit could have bagged Rosecrans's army and could perhaps have forced Abraham Lincoln to consider a negotiated peace with the Confederacy. But Bragg seemed stunned by the victory and let the Federals slip away. After the double Southern losses at Vicksburg and Gettysburg, Chickamauga raised Confederate spirits, but Bragg had really gained very little while losing a golden opportunity. Rosecrans had lost sixteen thousand of sixty thousand troops, but once he had reached Chattanooga he would quickly receive enough reinforcements to compensate. Bragg had lost seventeen thousand of his sixty-five thousand men who could not easily be replaced. But Bragg and the South had also lost the last opportunity to win the war.

Georgia monument, Chickamauga

Brotherton House, Chickamauga

Chickamauga Creek

Florida monument, Chickamauga

Tennessee River, seen from Lookout Mountain in Chickamauga and Chattanooga National Military Park, Tennessee

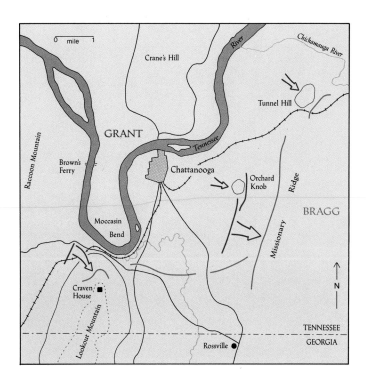

Chattanooga TENNESSEE

NOVEMBER 23–25, 1863

AFTER HIS BARREN VICTORY at Chickamauga, Braxton Bragg decided to besiege the battered Army of the Cumberland that had limped into Chattanooga. James Longstreet's wing occupied the area around Lookout Mountain, a rocky ridge fifteen hundred feet high that lay southwest of Chattanooga. Leonidas Polk deployed his right wing southeast of the city along Missionary Ridge, a spine two hundred feet high that ran southwest to northeast. Bragg hoped to block the Union supply line and to starve William Rosecrans's army into submission. To accomplish this task, Bragg had to control the Tennessee River where it looped through Chattanooga. But this strategy had a flaw: the siege operations took time that Bragg did not have.

Thousands of Federal reinforcements were pouring into Chattanooga. George Thomas took over the army from Rosecrans, who had fallen into disfavor after Chickamauga. U. S. Grant, the new commander of all Union forces in the west, arrived with men from Vicksburg and took personal charge of the situation at Chattanooga. Grant's trusted lieutenant, William T. Sherman, was on hand, and Joe Hooker arrived with parts of two corps detached from the Army of the Potomac.

Grant wasted no time. Hooker surprised Longstreet with an attack near Lookout Mountain and captured Brown's Ferry on the Tennessee. Now Grant could bring supplies from the west over Raccoon Mountain, across a pontoon bridge at the ferry, and into Chattanooga across a strip of land where the Tennessee curved down to Lookout and then away from it (the river route here was called Moccasin Bend).

Not long after Hooker's victory, Longstreet departed with his men to the northeast to attack Knoxville, currently occupied by Union forces under Ambrose Burnside. Richmond authorities believed that, if Longstreet could whip Burnside and then move west toward Nashville, Grant might be compelled to abandon Chattanooga. More realistically, Longstreet and Bragg wanted to be rid of one another, and Robert E. Lee wanted Longstreet closer to Virginia. Still, Bragg should have objected to a decision that deprived him of several thousand men. After all, he knew that Grant's force was steadily growing. In November, when Grant decided to break the siege, he had more than sixty thousand effectives, while Bragg's strength had shrunk to thirty-seven thousand.

The main thrust of Grant's plan was to be an assault by Sherman on the northeast end of Missionary Ridge. Thomas would keep Polk guessing by moving against the front of the ridge. But the Tennessee River current ripped away the Brown's Ferry pontoon, leaving part of Sherman's force behind, near Lookout Mountain. Grant decided to make the most of the situation. He gave Hooker one of Sherman's divisions and ordered him to prepare for an offensive against the Rebels on the mountain.

On Monday, November 23, Grant set his plans into motion by sending Thomas on a sortie toward Missionary Ridge. There had been rumors of a Confederate withdrawal, and Grant wanted to determine the facts. Thomas's divisions advanced and overwhelmed a few hundred Confederate pickets in the Battle of Orchard Knob, so named for a hill at the north end of the Confederate skirmish line. The ground Thomas took proved to be a valuable staging area for future operations.

The next day Grant ordered attacks on both Rebel flanks. Sherman's troops swept up what they thought was the north end of Missionary Ridge only to find that they were on another ridge in front of Missionary. There they encountered Pat Cleburne's Confederate division, a band of fighters second to none in any army. Cleburne had entrenched on Tunnel Hill, which dotted the "I" of Missionary Ridge. Sherman attacked and was stopped cold by Cleburne.

On Lookout Mountain, Joe Hooker had a better Tuesday than Sherman. His ten thousand men faced fewer than three thousand Confederates who were not prepared to withstand an assault. Decisive fighting took place around the Craven House, where the Confederates had built log and stone breastworks. Confederate General Carter Stephenson had been sent the night before to take over this command. He knew nothing of the situation and did not have time to learn. Still, his men put up a good fight. Their success was limited principally by Hooker's overwhelming numbers. If Longstreet had still been on hand, things might have turned out differently. As it was, Hooker easily won the so-called Battle above the Clouds.

On Wednesday, November 25, Sherman sent six divisions against Cleburne, but the Confederates held firm. The fighting raged for hours. On the steeper slopes, Cleburne's men rained boulders down on the Yankees and threw cannonballs as if they were hand grenades. Joe Hooker, who had been expected to hit Polk's left to take the pressure off Sherman, never appeared. Grant therefore ordered Thomas to move against the face of Missionary Ridge. Thomas's men were to try to take the Confederate trenches in front of the base of the ridge. That mission accomplished, they were to halt and await further orders. It was hoped that the diversion would allow Sherman to break Cleburne's defense.

Once Thomas's offensive got under way, it kept going. Thomas and Grant watched transfixed as the mass of men

Battle above the Clouds, Chattanooga

in blue reached the base of the ridge and began climbing it. Bragg had established a second line of defense, and the Confederates on this front poured a murderous fire into the oncoming Yankees. Thomas's men seemed to reach the same conclusion all at once. The safest way to go was up. The other choices were to stay pinned down or to be shot while retreating.

Up the face of Missionary Ridge came the Federal wave. Confederates were shocked that anyone would try such a thing. Shooting straight down the sheer drop was a necessary but difficult task with rifles and impossible with artillery. The attack fractured Bragg's second line and came on up. Confederates at the crest fought for a while but finally panicked and ran. Many reasons have been given for the disintegration of Bragg's lines on the ridge. Psychologically the Confederates had been adversely affected by the thousands of reinforcements clearly visible on the valley floor below.

Perhaps, too, the élan of the army had deteriorated after so many weeks of inactivity. The best explanation seems to be that Bragg and his generals, confident that the ridge was impregnable, had prepared very inadequate defenses. The crest of the ridge was especially poorly entrenched.

Saved from further humiliation by Cleburne's solid rearguard defense, Bragg's army streamed to the south, minus some sixty-seven hundred casualties (two-thirds of whom were captured). Grant had lost some fifty-eight hundred men and had gained control of the gateway to Atlanta and other points south. More fighting lay ahead, and the Army of Tennessee would have opportunities to redeem itself. It had not run from a fight before and would not do so again. The morale of the army received a major boost when Joseph E. Johnston replaced Bragg. But Bragg's poor performance had already cost the Confederacy more than it could recover.

West Run, Chattanooga

Lookout Mountain, Chattanooga

Sherman Reservation on Missionary Ridge, Chattanooga

Ohio Reservation on Missionary Ridge (above) and Moccasin Bend (following pages), Chattanooga

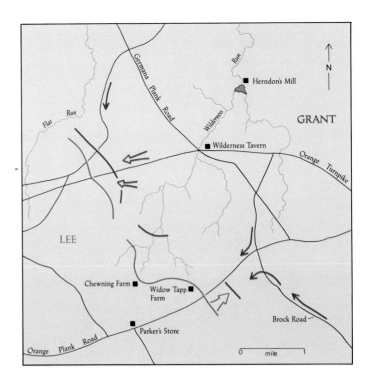

Wilderness VIRGINIA

May 5–6, 1864

THE VIRGINIA CAMPAIGN of 1864 got under way in early May. U. S. Grant had left Tennessee to assume command of all Federal forces. Grant came up with a simple plan. George Meade's 120,000-man Army of the Potomac would move south to Richmond. General Benjamin Butler would take a smaller force of 35,000 and ascend the James River to attack Richmond from the southeast. Butler immediately took himself out of the campaign when he advanced and then retreated to a strip of land between the Appomattox River and the James. P. G. T. Beauregard, commanding a Richmond army of 25,000, threw entrenchments across the neck of this peninsula. There Butler was, as Grant said, like "a bottle strongly corked."

Grant traveled with Meade's army and in effect gave the orders. Robert E. Lee's Army of Northern Virginia was deployed east to west from a dense forest near Chancellorsville called the Wilderness to Orange Court House to Gordonsville. Grant decided to move toward Lee's right flank in the Chancellorsville/Wilderness area in an attempt to cut the Confederate army off from Richmond.

When Lee realized what was afoot, he sent the corps of A. P. Hill and Richard Ewell hurrying toward the Wilderness. Ewell marched down the Orange

Turnpike while Hill took the parallel Orange Plank Road just south of Ewell. Lee hoped Hill and Ewell could hold out until James Longstreet arrived from Gordonsville. Lee wanted to make his fight at the Wilderness because the impenetrable thickets there would negate Grant's superiority in numbers.

Shortly before noon on Thursday, May 5, the right wing of Meade's army was moving southeastward into the Wilderness and met Ewell's corps coming down the Orange Turnpike. The Yankees immediately attacked. About the same time Federal cavalry attacked Hill's troops to the south. At the time Hill and Ewell were some three miles apart and not able to communicate. Undaunted, Hill rushed his corps toward the Brock Road. He hoped to cut in behind Winfield Hancock's corps, which was already moving south past the intersection of the Brock and Orange Plank roads. Hill could then turn north and hit the left flank of Gouverneur Warren's corps, which was strung out north to south, fighting Ewell. The combined Confederate forces could quickly dispose of Warren and then pursue an isolated Hancock.

Meade saw that his right wing was in danger of being split and rushed part of John Sedgwick's corps to the crossroads. Hancock received orders to

countermarch and support Sedgwick. The Federals won the race to the crossing. Hill deployed his men on the Widow Tapp's farm west of Brock Road and extended his left to the north in a vain attempt to link with Ewell's right.

The fighting on both fronts evolved into a confused series of advances and retreats. In the tangled Wilderness growth, soldiers were guided by sound more than by sight. Men on both sides fired repeatedly at unseen enemies. Ewell and Warren struggled to a stalemate, but the battle on Hill's front was more desperate because of the road junction's strategic importance. Hancock moved up from the south to the plank road, wheeled left, and joined in the assault on Hill. The battlefield became a place of teror. Wounded men burned to death in underbrush fires set by exploding artillery shells. Breastworks caught fire, and men only a few yards apart on each side shot at each other through the blaze. The Wilderness was truly hell to fight in.

With Hancock now up, Hill faced nearly three times his number. Although his line held stubbornly, by evening his men had been battered to the breaking point. While Hill directed his troops, he kept looking over his shoulder for Longstreet. At last the fighting stopped for the night after a guard detail of 125 Alabamians yelled like demons and bluffed the Union division of James Wadsworth into halting a flank attack that would probably have broken Hill's line.

During the night, the naturally low visibility of the Wilderness was compounded by the pall of smoke from wood fires. The scent of burning flesh permeated the air, and the screams of the wounded echoed through the darkness. It was almost impossible to reform lines, and so most men stayed where they were. Longstreet finally arrived about 5:00 A.M., May 6, but his corps was still back down the trail. As he discussed the situation with Hill, the Federals came crashing through the thickets.

All along the line a sea of blue brigades smashed into Hill's ill-prepared Confederates. The Rebels retreated slowly but in good order. Hill's veterans were terrific fighters, and as Lee had expected, the dense woods slowed and confused the Yankee attack. The Wilderness had indeed proved a great equalizer. On Hill's left, Wadsworth's troops became entangled with David Birney's division, and Hill personally helped man the cannon that sent charge after charge of canister into the Federal mass. At that moment, Longstreet's vanguard appeared.

Lee now had nearly his whole army of seventy-five thousand on hand or near the battlefield. Longstreet deployed his division and charged. Gradually he

shifted his attack to the right while Hill spread his men to the left. The extension of the lines thwarted Federal attempts to get between Hill and Ewell. Now Hill charged as Longstreet pressured Hancock's left. By the time the fighting ended, the Confederates had taken back lost ground. Near where Stonewall Jackson had fallen a year earlier, Longstreet too was struck by accidental fire from his own men. Lee's old warhorse survived but would be out of action for several months. Richard Anderson took over Longstreet's corps.

To the north, Dick Ewell spent the sixth checking attempts to turn his flanks. Late in the day he sent John Gordon's division to hit Warren's exposed right flank. The assault carried the Federal trenches and then ground to a halt. Ewell had accomplished little more than shoring up his lines.

The Battle of the Wilderness was over. Both Grant and Lee had courted disaster during the two-day struggle. Casualties had been quite high on both sides. Grant lost 16,000 and Lee 11,500. Lee's lines had held against superior numbers. Usually after such a pounding the Confederates could expect the Army of the Potomac to slink back to Washington. But Lee's fears were borne out. Abraham Lincoln had found a general who would not retreat readily. Grant had been checked by Lee, but the Federal army would keep going south, regardless of the cost. The war would not end until one side or the other could no longer fight.

*Wilderness Run, Wilderness Battlefield in Fredericksburg and Spotsylvania Court House National Military Park,
Virginia*

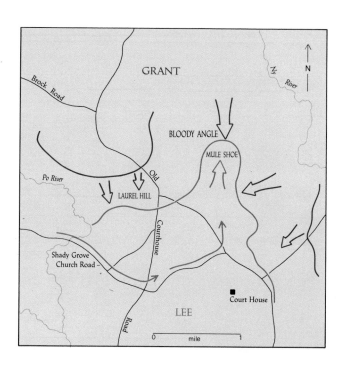

Spotsylvania   VIRGINIA

MAY 8–21, 1864

LEAVING THE SMOLDERING WILDERNESS behind, U. S. Grant set his sights on the village of Spotsylvania Court House to the southeast. It was not much of a settlement, but the intersection there of several roads made it of strategic importance in Grant's continuing effort to cut Robert E. Lee off from Richmond. Lee knew that he had to reach Spotsylvania first and pushed his army accordingly. Grant also urged his army onward. The Federals might have won the race had not a ludicrous fistfight developed between veteran and rookie cavalrymen over fresh horses. The incident occurred near the head of the Federal column, and delayed the army for more than an hour, just enough time for Lee's van to reach Spotsylvania first.

The Confederates hurriedly established a line of battle that formed an arc some six miles long, facing north and northeast. A. P. Hill's corps, temporarily led by Jubal Early because Hill continued to have health problems, manned the right flank. Richard Ewell held the center, and Richard Anderson (Longstreet's corps) held the left. At the center of the line, trenches bulged to cover high ground, forming a salient known as the mule shoe.

Grant's army finally arrived with Gouverneur Warren's corps in the lead, followed by John Sedgwick and Winfield Hancock. Ambrose Burnside soon came up on the left by a separate route. Hancock held the center of Grant's line, with Sedgwick and Warren on the right and Burnside remaining on the left.

The initial phases of the battle began on Sunday, May 8, with much skirmishing and jockeying for position. The battles fought were isolated in the sense that the armies did not come together in one gigantic clash. John Sedgwick fell dead from a sniper's bullet during the fighting at an area called Laurel Hill. Horatio Wright replaced Sedgwick, whom Grant mourned as more valuable than a division. On May 10, Henry Heth's division made a sortie down Shady Grove Church Road and drove Federals back beyond the Po River on the Rebel left.

On May 10, Union general Emory Upton attacked the west side of the mule shoe en masse with several brigades. The idea was that sheer force might break this vulnerable spot in Lee's lines. The initial assault succeeded, but with heavy casualties. Yankees in the forefront of the attack fell, shot through the head by Rebels standing erect behind the high breastworks. Bitter hand-to-hand fighting erupted, and Confederate reinforcements finally drove Upton back to Union lines. Although the attack failed, the tactic showed promise, so Grant made plans to try again, this time with Hancock's full corps, supported on the right and left by Wright and Burnside, respectively.

Robert E. Lee inadvertently played straight into Grant's hands. Union wagons had been spotted off to the northeast, and Lee supposed that the Army of the Potomac had begun shifting left in another attempt to turn his right. Consequently twenty-two artillery pieces that formed the bulwark of the mule shoe's defense were pulled back to be transferred for use in the next confrontation.

On the foggy morning of Thursday, May 12, at 4:35 A.M., Francis Barlow's division of Hancock's corps marched toward the salient. The blue wave hit Lee's line and crumpled it. Confederate officers, sensing trouble, had sent word that the artillery should be rushed back to the front. But the pieces arrived too late, several were captured, and they would have been better off left in the rear. Without the guns, rebels swung muskets as clubs and flashed bayonets in a vain effort to stop the Yankee assault.

The divisions of Barlow and David Birney bagged several thousand prisoners from Ewell's corps, but Lee rushed forward reinforcements who managed to stem the tide and drive the Federals back. Union soldiers retreated only as far as the mule shoe trenches, where they turned and made a stand. There was much confusion because Hancock had thousands of soldiers crowded into a very small area, and the attack itself had gotten divisions all mixed up together.

But there was not much time to reorganize or even to think about the fight developing on the northwest angle of the salient. Confederates piled into the area, battle flags waved on both sides of the trenches, and there was probably never any worse face-to-face fighting in this or any other war. From the front back to the rear on each side, men were packed several ranks deep. The trenches became piled high with dead and wounded. Loaded rifles were passed to men on the front lines. They fired until they were shot down, and then the next shooters stepped up. Rain began to fall, and still the firing continued. Men continued to die, and more men certain to be shot marched up to take their turn. Water filled the trenches and carried away blood but could not erase the horror of what soldiers called the "Bloody Angle." Bullets flew so thickly that Confederate general Sam McGowan saw an oak tree two feet thick cut down by lead missiles. The continual musketry ripped apart bodies already dead. When the stacks of fallen soldiers grew too high, corpses were tossed aside. The fighting never missed a beat.

To the rear of the carnage, Confederates worked desperately to establish a new line. At midnight they finally finished. The Rebels pulled back, and the fighting was mercifully over. Lee's line had held by the thinnest of margins, thanks not only to the bravery of men in the salient but to the repulse by the rest of his army of the flank offensive by Burnside and Wright.

Morning came, and men who viewed the Bloody Angle never forgot what they saw. All around lay mutilated bodies and stacks of corpses. There was an occasional moan from those of the wounded who had somehow escaped suffocation at the bottom of piles of bodies. The scene attested to the heroism of both armies and to the insanity of war. One soldier remarked that he would never lose patience with those who would not believe his description of the Angle. Had he not seen it himself, he would not have believed it.

The armies stared at each other for several more days, did some more fighting, and then moved south again. Grant's casualty lists were growing. He had lost some thirty-five thousand men so far. But replacements were arriving, and he was determined to keep going and to keep fighting even if it took, as he said, "all summer."

Lee was losing men, too, but his could not be replaced. He had lost some ten thousand at the Bloody Angle alone, and it did not help at all to know that Grant had lost just as many. The Confederate army was melting away, and so were Lee's trusted lieutenants. First Jackson had been killed, then Longstreet severely wounded, and now J. E. B. Stuart had been killed on May 11 while fighting Phil Sheridan's cavalry at Yellow Tavern north of Richmond. For Lee, the road south was becoming a death march.

Federals' pontoon bridge over the North Anna River shortly after Spotsylvania Battle

GENERALS HANCOCK AND WRIGHT FIGHTING FOR THE ENEMY'S RIFLE-PITS.

Bloody Angle, the Salient, Spotsylvania Court House in Fredericksburg and Spotsylvania Court House National Military Park (above and left)

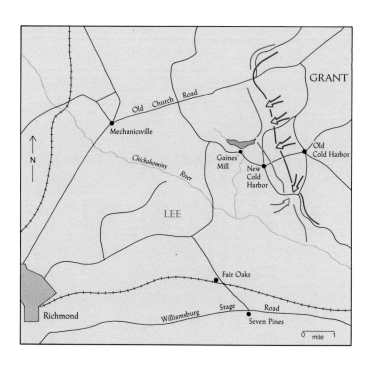

Cold Harbor   VIRGINIA

JUNE 1–3, 1864

AFTER THE ARMY OF THE POTOMAC moved away from Spotsylvania, Robert E. Lee ordered the Army of Northern Virginia to retreat to the North Anna River. The position was only twenty-five miles north of Richmond, but it would enable Lee to protect vital railroads. On May 22, part of A. P. Hill's corps attacked Gouverneur Warren's corps on the south bank of the North Anna. Little came of the fight, which was mild by comparison with the engagements of recent weeks, except that Grant was persuaded to make his next stand elsewhere.

The Federal columns moved to the left once more. Once more the Confederates moved right to stay between the Yankees and Richmond. Grant's next target was the Chickahominy River at a point ten miles east of the Rebel capitol. Sporadic fighting erupted, and the shifting continued until the six-mile-long battle lines ran north and south. The Confederates faced east, with Richard Ewell's corps divided to cover the flanks and with Hill and Richard Anderson in between. The southern flank of each army was anchored on the Chickahominy.

Lee knew that if Grant decided to mount a major attack here it would come at the right center of the Confederate line near Cold Harbor, which was neither a harbor nor cold but merely a spot where several roads intersected. Both armies needed Cold Harbor to control future movements in the campaign. Grant shifted Horatio Wright's corps from the Union right over to the left to keep the crossroads free of Rebels. (It was normal marching procedure in the Federal army to shift corps from one end of the line to the other in order to guard against flank attacks.) To assist Wright, Baldy Smith's corps was transferred by water from Benjamin Butler's bottled-up army below Richmond.

On Wednesday, June 1, the Federals attacked and pushed the Rebel line west of Cold Harbor. But the push did not carry very far, and if Grant intended to secure the crossroads, more fighting would be necessary. Grant prepared for more by bringing up Winfield Hancock's corps to join in the next assault scheduled for June 2. But Thursday came and went quietly. The giant Union army spent the day marching and countermarching and shifting to and fro, trying to find a position from which to attack. All the while, no one bothered to check the terrain in front of the lines, terrain that Lee's men had turned into an intricate pattern of impressive entrenchments that would offer attackers the prospect of suicide. Every nook and cranny of ground had been adapted to defensive advantage so that an assaulting force would be vulnerable front and flank.

At 4:30 A.M. on Friday, June 3, Hancock, Wright, and Smith moved forward. In their front waited most of Hill's corps and half of Anderson's, fifty thousand Federals against thirty thousand Confederates. Thousands of rifles cracked, hundreds of cannon roared, and a thick fog shrouded the spectacle.

First the Union corps, then divisions, and finally brigades became separated as the hot Rebel fire from the labyrinth of trenches fragmented the Federal attack. Grant had wanted this fight because he was tired of maneuvering and because Richmond was so close, but the charge was pure madness. Yankees fell in droves; whole companies hit the dust dead and wounded as Lee's veterans turned the affair into a turkey shoot. One Federal officer described the Confederate fire as "more like a volcanic blast than a battle, and . . . just about as destructive." In response to an inquiry from Lee about how the battle was proceeding on his front, Hill showed the messenger the mass of Union dead piled in front of his trenches.

Union trench, Cold Harbor Battlefield in Richmond National Battlefield Park, Virginia

In half an hour the slaughter was over. Seven thousand Union soldiers lay in front of Lee's line. A Rebel officer commented, "It was not war. It was murder." Lee's fifteen hundred casualties were minuscule by comparison. Grant had taken a profound beating, but he would not leave. The Federals dug in and waited. Men in the trenches grew impatient, but it was certain death to venture out. In fact, no one could stand erect and hope to live. Days passed and in the hot Virginia sun dead bodies decomposed rapidly. Finally, on June 7, Grant agreed to a burial truce that made Cold Harbor a little more bearable for the living.

Grant soon decided to abandon the position and move southeast again. Lee could not be driven out of his trenches; the June 3 debacle had proved that point. So on June 12 the Army of the Potomac moved out toward Petersburg south of Richmond. Lee was taken by surprise, since most of his cavalry was scouting elsewhere to protect his supply lines. Once more the Army of Northern Virginia was in a race. This time the goal was Petersburg where it would try again to save the Confederacy.

Kennesaw Mountain National Battlefield Park, Georgia

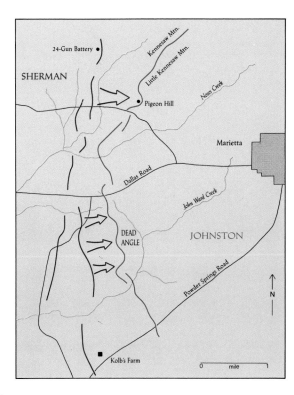

Kennesaw Mountain   GEORGIA

June 22–27, 1864

WHEN U. S. GRANT went east to assume command of all Federal armies, he placed his trusted lieutenant, William T. Sherman, in command of Union forces in the west. While Grant hammered away at Robert E. Lee, Sherman went after the Confederate Army of Tennessee, commanded by Joseph E. Johnston. Sherman adopted the same type of sidewheeling maneuver as Grant, except that Sherman continuously tried to turn Johnston's left. Like Lee, Johnston had an important city to protect, in this case Atlanta.

One factor that concerned Sherman was that, as he proceeded southward into Georgia, his supply lines would become more and more vulnerable. Nathan Bedford Forrest particularly worried Sherman. Forrest had been sent west with his cavalry, where he roamed about Mississippi, Alabama, and West Tennessee. To keep him busy, two expeditions were sent against him from Memphis into north Mississippi. On June 10, 1864, Forrest scored one of the most magnificent victories of the war at Brice's Crossroads when he defeated a Federal column nearly three times his number. On July 14–15, Forrest and Stephen D. Lee were beaten at the Battle of Tupelo, but they held their position, and the Yankee expedition

retreated back to Memphis. So Forrest remained free, but the raids kept him away from Sherman, and Richmond authorities wasted his considerable talents by not ordering him to Georgia.

Sherman's campaign began southeast of Chattanooga near Dalton, Georgia, in early May 1864, progressed south and southeast toward Atlanta and forced Johnston to begin a series of retreats. The Federals marched into Georgia some one hundred thousand strong, while Johnston had about sixty-five thousand men. Forced out of Dalton, Johnston met Sherman at Resaca on May 14–15, where an indecisive battle was fought. North of Cassville, Sherman spread his front from east to west and moved south. Johnston intended to challenge the Yankee advance by hitting the exposed Union left, but the assault misfired, and Sherman again swung to his right, forcing Johnston to fall back. At New Hope Church on May 25–28, Sherman failed in an attempt to turn the Rebel right and repelled an attack on his own right.

Finally Sherman abandoned the field and moved eastward around Johnston's right toward the Western and Atlantic Railroad that ran northwest out of Atlanta. Johnston shifted first to Pine Mountain, where Leonidas Polk was

killed by an artillery shell. Then Johnston moved to Kennesaw Mountain, a seven-hundred-foot eminence some two and one-half miles long that stood four miles north of Marietta. Johnston occupied strong entrenchments that ran from the south to the northeast. William Hardee's corps held the left of the line, while Polk's former corps, temporarily led by William W. Loring, held the center and John Bell Hood the right. The fortifications and the steep elevation of Kennesaw's slopes made it unlikely that Sherman would attack.

For several days the Union army moved along the Confederate front as Sherman pondered his next move. Once again he pushed against Johnston's left. Johnston countered by moving Hood's corps from right to left. On June 22, Hood lunged at Joe Hooker's corps, but reinforcements drove the Confederates back.

The whole business had long since settled into a methodical boxing match, with both sides carefully punching and counterpunching. Johnston had pretty much stayed on the defensive, which was his forte, and in the process had managed to negate Sherman's numerical superiority to a large extent. Now here, before the heights of Kennesaw Mountain, Sherman abandoned

Kennesaw Mountain in 1864

maneuver and went for the jugular. He figured that Johnston would be anticipating more flank moves, so with the advantage of surprise, a charge at the enemy's center might succeed. The idea was reminiscent of Pickett at Gettysburg and Grant at Cold Harbor. If Johnston's men were alert, the results would be equally disastrous.

Early on Monday, June 27, Sherman's artillery opened up a barrage intended to soften Johnston's breastworks. Then the Federals charged. John Schofield's Army of the Ohio advanced on Johnston's left, James McPherson's Army of the Tennessee hit the Rebel right, and George Thomas's Army of the Cumberland launched the main attack against William Hardee's corps in the center.

The Confederates had not been caught napping. A "withering fire" greeted the Yankees, who "sought shelter behind logs and rocks." In some horrendous respects, the fight for Kennesaw was a combination of the Wilderness and Spotsylvania. Some of the bloodiest fighting between Polk's and Thomas's men raged around a Confederate salient that earned the name "Dead Angle." From behind log breastworks, Ben Cheatham's Rebel division poured rifle fire into the attacking Federals. In the whirlwind of lead and iron, a Tennessean could be heard yelling appropriately, "Hell has broke loose in Georgia." The day was indeed unmercifully hot. The temperature rose to 110 degrees, and exploding shells set the surrounding woods on fire. A truce was hurriedly called by Rebels so that Yankees could

rescue wounded comrades from the blaze.

By 11:30 A.M. Sherman's army was retreating back down the mountain. One of Thomas's corps commanders summed up the morning's action: "Our losses in this assault were heavy indeed, and our gain was nothing." Sherman had lost three thousand men and had nothing to show for it. Johnston had suffered only five or six hundred casualties.

Sherman was philosophical. He figured he had taught his men that strong fortifications must sometimes be attacked regardless of the cost. He had also shown the Confederates that he was capable of all-out assaults. Sherman was probably just being defensive. He had not taught men in either army anything they had not already learned. The foolishness of the Kennesaw attack was soon demonstrated by Sherman himself as he once more wheeled to his right, forcing Johnston to retreat. With Atlanta as his immediate goal and several routes available to get there, Sherman had the ability, before and after the battle, to maneuver Johnston off the Kennesaw position.

Johnston kept retreating until an exasperated Jefferson Davis replaced him with John Bell Hood. More a fighter than a tactician, Hood assailed

Sherman's army in several bloody fights around Atlanta. In the end, Hood decimated his ranks, withdrew from Atlanta, and headed north for his infamous Tennessee campaign, where disastrous defeats at Franklin and Nashville reduced his army to a shadow of its former self. Sherman marched to Savannah, leaving a path of devastation in his wake, and then in the spring of 1865 moved up the Atlantic coast into North Carolina. There he met Johnston, who had been restored to command of the last remnants of the Army of Tennessee. On March 19, 1865, Johnston attacked Sherman and after two days of fighting was defeated at Bentonville, North Carolina. After learning that Robert E. Lee had surrendered in Virginia, Johnston capitulated and, on April 18, four days after Abraham Lincoln had been assassinated, met with Sherman at the Bennett house near Durham Station to sign a surrender document. A new agreement had to be signed on April 26 after Washington authorities rejected Sherman's terms as too liberal and argued that they exceeded his authority. And so the war came to an end for the two primary armies of the western theater, ironically in the east at a place 125 miles south of Appomattox Court House, Virginia.

Granite top of Kennesaw Mountain

Kennesaw Mountain, Georgia

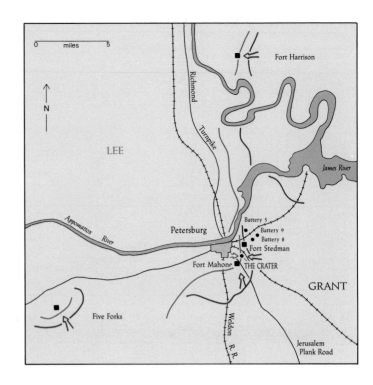

Petersburg   VIRGINIA

JUNE 15, 1864–APRIL 2, 1865

U. S. GRANT MOVED the Army of the Potomac from Cold Harbor across the rivers east of Richmond and marched south of the Confederate capital toward Petersburg, where he intended to cut Virginia's supply line from the Carolinas. Petersburg had a myriad of well-constructed trenches but, except for local militia, precious few soldiers to defend the city. On June 9, these defenders had beaten off an attack by elements of Benjamin Butler's army, but they could not begin to match Grant's masses.

On June 15, Winfield Hancock's corps (temporarily led by David Birney) and Baldy Smith's corps of Butler's army poised to attack Petersburg's outer defenses. P. G. T. Beauregard left Richmond with as many men as could be spared and hurried southward. He arrived in time to help slow the Federal attack, which never fulfilled expectations and succeeded in capturing only about a mile of Rebel works. Two more days passed, and by then most of Grant's army had reached Petersburg. Although Beauregard's small force was obliged to concede peripheral trenches, the men fought magnificently and held on. By June 18, Lee and the Army of Northern Virginia had arrived, and Grant had squandered his best opportunity thus far in the campaign. Grant's army needed a rest, and Lee

was forced to stay where he was to protect supply lines. Grant therefore decided to besiege Petersburg. Unlike his Vicksburg operations, Grant's Petersburg siege did not involve encircling a whole town. The Federal front ran from northeast of Petersburg southward in a long arc. All Grant had to do was to keep extending his line to the south, thereby forcing Lee to stretch his already thin ranks again and again. Grant already controlled two railroads and several roads on the east side of the battlefront. Lee had said at the beginning of this campaign that he could not be maneuvered into a siege and survive. There was nothing to do now but hope that his 50,000 could somehow work a miracle against Grant's 110,000.

Despite the odds, Grant quickly learned that the Confederates had plenty of fight left. On June 22, A. P. Hill hit Birney's and Horatio Wright's corps as the Federals struggled to extend their lines in the area of Jerusalem Plank Road. The surprised Yankees fled in confusion, and William Mahone's division of Hill's corps took nearly two thousand prisoners.

A lull followed Hill's attack as both sides settled into the monotony of siege warfare. In addition to dodging bullets and shells, men battled summer heat and dust. Pennsylvanians who had been

coal miners before marching off to war proposed digging a tunnel underneath a Rebel salient east of Petersburg. Explosives would be placed in the tunnel, the salient would be blown apart, and Lee's line would be breached. Grant may have been skeptical, but he too was tired of the siege, and so he approved the project.

Some four hundred miners began digging. As the weeks went by, the shaft extended beyond a depth of five hundred feet. The increase in activity in the area made Lee suspicious. His engineers sank several shafts in a vain search for tunnels. By late July, the project was nearly complete. To expand the impact of the explosion, additional tunnels were dug at ninety-degree angles from the end of the main shaft.

At dawn on July 30, the charges were detonated. The ground rocked as if from an earthquake. The surface suddenly exploded, carrying Confederate artillery and several companies of South Carolinians skyward. The blast created a hole one hundred seventy feet long, seventy feet wide, and thirty feet deep. Federal columns waiting to charge stood transfixed for several minutes watching the spectacle, precious minutes that gave A. P. Hill time to shift troops to plug the gap.

The Union attack moved forward and deteriorated as soldiers acted more like

Union camp of heavy artillery on the way to Petersburg, Virginia

tourists than like an army given a chance to whip the enemy. Division commanders stood idly by as troops milled about. Meanwhile, Hill arrived and led a counterattack. Bloody fighting erupted, and the Rebels pushed on toward the rim of what became known as "The Crater." Much of the combat was hand to hand as blue and gray kicked, clubbed, and boxed all around and inside the crater.

The tide turned against the Yankees, who began running back to the safety of their own lines. Those who did not, including several black soldiers who had been fighting with much courage and tenacity, were not treated kindly by Hill's men. Fearing heavy casualties that might lead to charges of bigotry, the Federal high command had refused to allow black troops to lead the charge into the crater. But after the assault had deteriorated, the troops had been sent forward into a hellish situation far worse than they would likely have encountered at the head of the attack. Infuriated by the explosion itself, the Confederates grew angrier when they saw former slaves shooting at them. Volleys of Rebel fire swept the crater as war became vengeance. The Confederates resecured their lines, and the siege once more settled into its dull routine.

In late September, a major action took place at Fort Harrison, an anchor of outer Confederate defenses east of Richmond and north of the James River. Grant ordered the attack to keep reinforcements from being sent to Jubal Early, who was fighting to protect the Shenandoah Valley from Federal cavalry. (Early had taken over the corps of Richard Ewell, who had received an injury at Spotsylvania and had never sufficiently recovered to tolerate the rigors of field command.) The surprise attack at Harrison by the corps of Birney and E. O. C. Ord on September 29 left the fort in Federal hands. Lee ordered a counterattack the next day which failed and forced the Confederates to pull their lines back closer to Richmond.

After taking Fort Harrison, Grant concentrated all his operations south of the James. Periodically he made attempts to cut the Weldon railroad south of Petersburg. Each attempt failed, but the continual pressure weakened Lee's right flank.

The siege dragged on into the fall and winter. Desertion became a major problem for Lee as many Confederates decided that the war had been lost and that it was time to go home. Spring of 1865 approached, and Lee knew that he had to do something. If the Federal line

were hit hard enough to force Grant to tighten his front, easing pressure on Lee's right, then Lee could pull out part of his army, move into North Carolina, join forces with Joe Johnston to whip William T. Sherman, and then return with Johnston to fight Grant. It was the longest of long shots, but it had to be tried.

So Lee chose a spot and ordered an attack on Fort Stedman, a position in the Federal line east of Petersburg and north of the crater. Stedman was not very formidable, but Ambrose Burnside, whose troops held the fort, were prepared for the attack in the early hours of March 25, 1865. The initial charge carried the Rebels right on past Stedman, but Union reinforcements and a counterattack forced a Confederate retreat.

Lee had made the effort, and he had failed. Time ran out on April 1. The Confederate right flank collapsed at the Battle of Five Forks. The next day Grant ordered a general assault. Lee pulled his army out of Petersburg and headed westward, leaving Richmond uncovered and forcing the Confederate government to retreat. During fighting on April 2, A. P. Hill was killed. It is somehow fitting that this Confederate warrior did not see the end of the Army of Northern Virginia, which had only a week to live.

Burrows of Grant's soldiers besieging Petersburg (right), Fort Stedman (below), and path to Meade Station, Battery 9 (across), Petersburg National Battlefield, Virginia

Site of Surrender, McLean House, Appomattox

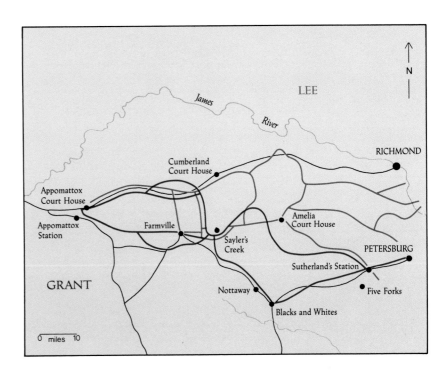

Appomattox

APRIL 9, 1865

AFTER LEAVING PETERSBURG, Robert E. Lee's army trekked westward. Lee intended to resupply his army at Amelia Court House, turn south, and join Joe Johnston. To prevent the junction with Johnston, U. S. Grant moved the Army of the Potomac on a parallel route south of Lee's march. Lee found no supplies at Amelia Court House. During the chaos of evacuating Richmond, no one in the government had seen to it that the supplies were shipped. The Army of Northern Virginia now lost valuable time as 'it moved on to Farmville in search of food.

On April 6 near the Appomattox River, the army divided as it prepared to cross the stream. In Sayler's Creek bottom, Richard Ewell found his corps cut off and surrounded. He had no choice but to surrender. Elements of other Confederate units were also captured, and in one blow Lee lost eight thousand men.

With the rest of the army safely across the Appomattox, Lee fought a delaying action while his army loaded up with supplies at Farmville. But it was too late. The delays and the Sayler's Creek disaster had given Grant time to cut off every route available to the Confederates. On April 9, Palm Sunday, the Rebel ranks, reduced now to fewer than thirty thousand, tried to break

through Federal lines posted west of Appomattox Court House. The attack failed, and Lee knew he must surrender.

Lee and Grant had been corresponding since April 7. Lee had tried to buy time by pinning Grant down on specific surrender terms. Time had run out now, and Lee would have to hope for the best. Members of his staff rode into Appomattox to pick a site for the conference with Grant. Wilmer McLean, who had moved from the Manassas area in 1861 to get away from the war, offered his house. The offer was accepted.

Dressed in a new uniform that he donned before dawn, Lee reached the McLean house at about 1:00 P.M. Grant, his uniform as slouchy as usual, arrived half an hour later. The two men conferred in the parlor, located in the left front part of the house. Several staff and other officers accompanied Grant. Lee had only one staff member present to record the proceedings.

The two veteran warriors discussed old times in the army. Talk of the business at hand seemed difficult for both. Lee finally broached the subject, and Grant assured his respected adversary that the Confederates would be asked merely to lay down their arms and to pledge not to fight until they were paroled. Lee agreed and asked that

the details be put in writing.

Grant chewed on a cigar as he wrote out terms even more generous than had been discussed. Lee and his officers could keep their sidearms, personal mounts, and baggage. Lee asked whether other soldiers could retain their horses and mules, most of which were privately owned and would be needed for spring plowing. Grant did not rewrite the surrender document but did instruct his officers to make such an allowance. Arrangements were also made to provide hungry Southerners with rations. Lee departed at about 3:00 P.M. He met with Grant the next day just east of the village to finalize details of the capitulation.

All in all the surrender was an atypical end to a bloody civil war. Grant apparently wanted to assure Lee and the South that the North preferred reconciliation to recrimination. The terms worked out at Appomattox, liberal but much less so than those that Sherman had originally given Johnston in North Carolina, were extended to the rest of the Confederacy. By the end of May all Confederates had stacked their arms.

Lee too had contributed to the healing process. Some of his officers suggested continuing the war by sending the army into the countryside

McLean House, rear view

as guerrilla fighters. Lee refused and in doing so perhaps saved the nation from a fate worse than the four years of devastation just concluded.

To be sure, bitterness prevailed for many years after the war. It was rooted in personal tragedies of the sort inevitably associated with war and in events such as the assassination of Abraham Lincoln five days after Appomattox and the imprisonment of Jefferson Davis from 1865 to 1867. But without the sagacity of Grant and Lee, true reunion could have taken much longer than it did. Time eventually brought old veterans to joint reunions, and all Americans came to realize that soldiers in blue and gray had consistently displayed both heroism and reckless abandon in defending what each side considered a just cause. In the process they had created for posterity a legacy that all Americans could accept with pride.

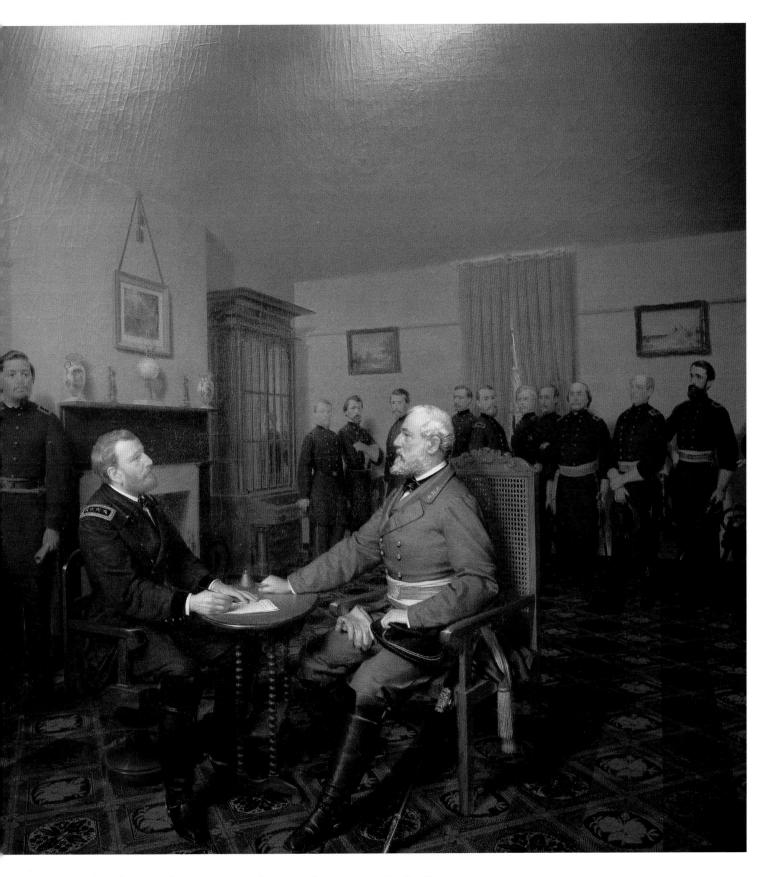

"Surrender of General Lee to General Grant" by Louis M.D. Guillaume,
Appomattox Court House, Virginia

For Further Reading

Each national Civil War park headquarters contains excellent brief studies of the local campaign and battle. Popularly written journals such as *Civil War Times Illustrated* and *Blue and Gray* periodically produce special issues on individual battles. These issues are often available at the appropriate parks.

The selected reading list below is a brief sampling of the available literature on the Civil War.

Bearss, Edwin C. *The Vicksburg Campaign*, 3 vols. Dayton, OH, 1985–87.

Carter, Samuel. *The Final Fortress: The Campaign for Vicksburg, 1862–1863*. New York, 1980.

Catton, Bruce. *The Centennial History of the Civil War*, 3 vols. Garden City, NY, 1961–1965.

———. *This Hallowed Ground: The Story of the Union Side of the Civil War*. Garden City, NY, 1956.

———. *A Stillness at Appomattox*. Garden City, NY, 1953.

Coddington, Edwin B. *The Gettysburg Campaign: A Study in Command*. New York, 1968.

Cooling, Benjamin Franklin. *Forts Henry and Donelson: The Key to the Confederate Heartland*. Knoxville, 1987.

Davis, William C. *Battle at Bull Run: A History of the First Major Campaign of the Civil War*. Garden City, NY, 1977.

Dowdy, Clifford. *The Seven Days: The Emergence of Lee*. Reprint. Wilmington, NC, 1988.

———. *Lee's Last Campaign: The Story of Lee and His Men Against Grant, 1864*. Boston, 1960.

Downey, Fairfax. *Storming of the Gateway: Chattanooga, 1863*. New York, 1960.

Foote, Shelby. *The Civil War: A Narrative*. 3 vols. New York, 1958–1974.

Jones, James Pickett and James Lee McDonough. *War So Terrible: Sherman and Atlanta*. New York, 1987.

McDonough, James Lee. *Chattanooga: A Death Grip on the Confederacy*. Knoxville, 1984.

———. *Shiloh: In Hell Before Night*. Knoxville, 1976.

———. *Stones River: Bloody Winter in Tennessee*. Knoxville, 1980.

Monaghan, Jay. *Civil War on the Western Border, 1854–1865*. Boston, 1955.

Sears, Stephen W. *Landscape Turned Red: The Battle of Antietam*. New Haven, CT, 1983.

Stackpoke, Edward J. *Drama on the Rappahannock: The Fredericksburg Campaign*. New York, 1957.

———. *Chancellorsville: Lee's Greatest Battle*. Harrisburg, PA, 1960.

Swanberg, William A. *First Blood: The Story of Fort Sumter*. New York, 1957.

Sword, Wiley. *Shiloh: Bloody April*. New York, 1974.

Tucker, Glenn. *Chickamauga: Bloody Battle in the West*. Indianapolis, IN, 1961.

———. *High Tide at Gettysburg: The Campaign in Pennsylvania*. Indianapolis, IN, 1958.